Earn $100 per day with Affiliate Marketing

What will we talk about in this guide:

1. What does affiliate marketing mean
2. How affiliate marketing works
3. 6 excellent reasons to become an affiliate
4. How much money can you actually make
5. How to start Affiliate Marketing with a website
6. How to start Affiliate Marketing without a website
7. How to find the products to promote
8. How to get traffic on your website using alternative methods
9. Alternatives to ClickBank
10. 12 essential tips to increase productivity
11. What is the fastest way to get started online
12. Keyword research: SEO competition analysis
13. 4 steps to find profitable affiliate niches
14. How to choose an affiliate program
15. What the market wants
16. Understanding of market interactions
17. 7 techniques on how to search for keywords
18. How to use Facebook
19. How to use Twitter
20. The importance of e-mail Marketing

PREFACE

Dear reader,
I thank you first of all for purchasing this guide, my goal is to guide you step by step to start working online, particularly in Affiliate Marketing.

In this guide you will learn what affiliate marketing is and how it works. You will also discover why it is FANTASTIC to be an affiliate, how much money you can make and how you can start.

I will try to be very basic in the explanation starting from the simple definition of Affiliate Marketing until you get to explain in detail all that you need and you do not have to do to start earning really in this reality.

I do not want to talk long, let's start right away. Enjoy the reading

1. What does affiliate marketing mean

Affiliate Marketing is a new way to make money online and it is an activity that is gaining more and more importance among young people.

By definition, affiliate marketing is:

"An Internet-based system where you (as an affiliate) are paid to report sales or customers to a company."

2. How affiliate marketing works

Affiliate marketing is one of the most efficient ways to make money online, where by promoting products or services, you earn a certain percentage as commission from sales made by you, through a special link that the marketer will give you after the registration. Sales are made on the web, through a website with banners, through promotional sites or through advertising campaigns.

This means that money is derived from sales of the promoted product. What you need to know is that the services or products you promote are provided by others and you, you only have to worry about the sale.

It is a bit like a real estate agent who does not own the houses he sells, but instead promotes houses on behalf of their clients and earn a percentage from the selling price of any property sold. Having said these, we now learn how to make money from affiliate marketing.

The image below shows a site with a banner that promotes a product, in this case a camera

Quale fotocamera compatta comprare

Molti smartphone sono in grado di scattare fotografie bellissime, ad altissima risoluzione e con colori brillanti. Però quando il gioco si fa duro, ossia quando bisogna scattare molte foto in un arco di tempo ristretto (es. in vacanza o durante una festa) e non si vuole correre il rischio di rimanere con la batteria a zero è meglio affidarsi a dispositivi ad hoc, come le fotocamere compatte. Dette anche **point and shoot**, uniscono la semplicità di utilizzo degli smartphone all'affidabilità delle macchine fotografiche tradizionali.

Non sono avanzate come le costosissime Reflex ma in contesti come quelli familiari o vacanzieri vanno più che bene (a meno che non si abbiano velleità di tipo artistico o professionale, questo è chiaro). Non per tutti i modelli valgono queste regole, però: negli ultimi anni si sono fatte avanti anche le cosiddette "compatte evolute", che uniscono al corpo minuscolo tipico delle point-and-shoot, una complessità nei comandi paragonabile a quella dei modelli di Reflex entry-level o di fascia media. La qualità è spesso inferiore, ma la comodità semplicemente non paragonabile.

When someone interested clicks on the banner, he is directed to the merchant's website.

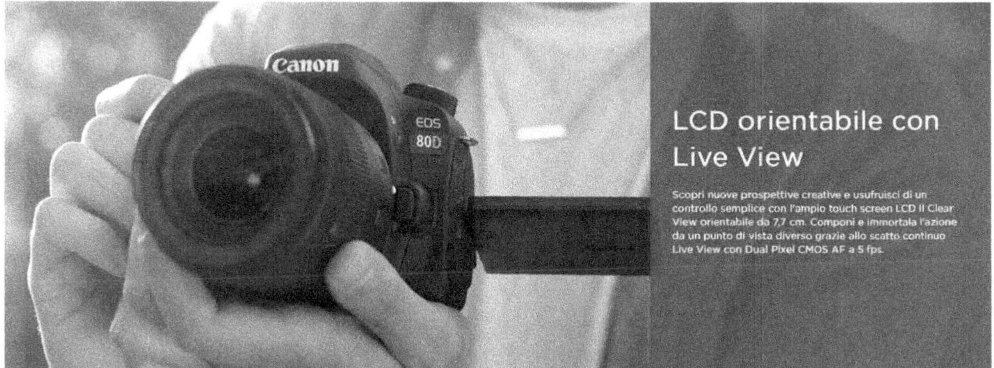

The trader is the person or company that creates and owns the product. Now it's up to the merchant to get that person to buy. If the person decides to purchase, the affiliate (you in this case) who sent them to the site earns a commission, which is a percentage of the selling price of the product. Simple, right?

There are several ways to place affiliate links on your website, one of the most popular ways to add links in addition to banners is to simply include them in your content.

If you have a site like this example that talks about cameras, you can link words with a link to your affiliate, which if clicked opens the page of your product.

3. 6 excellent reasons to become an affiliate

1. **Startup costs are very low**. To start a regular business in which you rent the retail space and inventory inventory, you could easily bring tens of thousands of dollars back. As an affiliate, you can start for the cost of a burger and fries.

2. **You do not need staff**. No more office politics and no manipulation of the disordered payroll. When you start as an affiliate you can do it all by yourself, and when it comes time to grow your business it's easy to outsource.

3. **You do not even need a product**. You simply have to promote products already on sale. Whether it's an eBook on training to keep fit or a camera, there's always a product that you can sell as an affiliate.

4. **You do not need any expert** knowledge to sell affiliate products. If you want to be an affiliate for weight loss products, then you do not need a Ph.D. in nutrition or exercise. All you need is a willing mentality to learn and the ability to market the right affiliate products to the right people.

5. **Earn a passive income**. It's a bit like the money you earn if you buy a house and then rent it - as long as you own that house and you're renting it, you earn money. In

a normal job you are paid only once for the work you do, but as an affiliate you can continue to earn from the same working day, every day, 24 hours a day.

6. **The opportunity to earn passively**. I'm not saying you'll be sitting on a beach drinking Piña Colada and you'll only work an hour a day after your first month as an affiliate. However, you have the power to work when you feel like it and have a more flexible life. You become the head of yourself - is not it beautiful?

4. How much money can you actually make

Like any real work, it all depends on how much effort you have put and how seriously you take it. For example, if you work only an hour a day, or spend most of your time checking emails instead of doing the work, then you may not make a lot of money.

But if you're really dedicated and treat your affiliate marketing as a real business, and if you get 100% every time you sit down from your computer, you can definitely get a **full-time income**.

Let's do some quick math on how much you can actually do as an affiliate. Imagine promoting "Singorama", a training course to learn how to sing very popular.

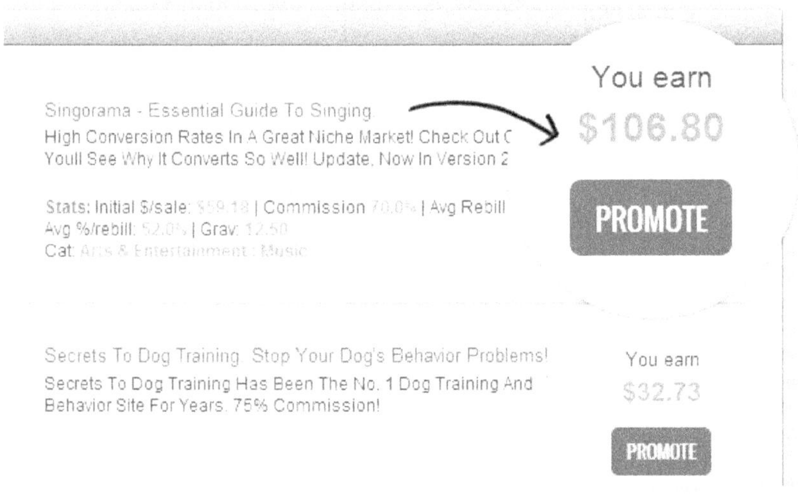

If you could only get ONE day sale of Singorama (and believe me when I say there are many affiliates who do a lot more than this), then you would make an extra $ 747.60 a week, which is $ 3,204 a month and $ 38,982 a year.

You will agree with me that it becomes a job in every respect and the earnings are excellent.

5. How to start Affiliate Marketing with a website

Now I'll give you an overview of the affiliate marketing process to get an idea of how everything works and then I'll give you an example to use as a reference.

It's important when learning about the whole process not to feel overwhelmed, so we're going to finish off with an outline of what you can get started with straight away. So let's dive in and discover what's involved.

The Process of Affiliate Marketing

1. Pick a topic

Firstly, pick a topic that you're interested in that also has a lot of market potential. Think of something that you like, and consider whether there would be many products associated with it, or much of an audience. You can find a topic (or "niche," as affiliates call it) with a little research..

2. Find products to promote

Once you've got a niche all picked out, find some products that you can promote. There are websites full of these (called affiliate networks) to browse, and you can find advice here on how to choose the best ones for you. Once you've got a couple that are right for you, you'll be able to get an affiliate link for them.

3. Build a website

Next up, you need to build a website! I thought this would be extremely confusing and difficult, but it really wasn't. WordPress and similar sites makes it super simple for anyone to build a quality website. (even to those who do not know anything about programming)

4. Fill your website with relevant content

Fill your website with content that will be useful to the people who are interested in your niche, and place your affiliate links throughout in the most relevant places. That way when someone interested in your content clicks your link, they go to a sales page for a product that they might also be interested in, and if they buy it you get a commission!

5. Promote your website

When you've set this up, all that's left to do is promote your website so you can get more people to your content, and more potential for commissions from referred sales. There are a lot of different marketing strategies out there, from advertising to social media, but you won't have to worry about this part of it straight away.

Example for Reference

Topic: Weight loss

Suppose, for example, that I have an interest In weight loss. I would do research on Google Trends using words related to my research, and in this case discover that there is a strong market interested in losing weight.

Find products on an affiliate network: ClickBank

Create an account on ClickBank and start selecting the products available based on your search.

Build a website: Hosting, domain name, and WordPress

Now you need a hosting provider (a place to put the website on the internet) and a domain name (ex: www.weightloss.com), then install WordPress so you can start playing with the appearance of the your website. There are many free themes for WordPress if you do not have a big chance, or if you can you can buy a high quality one.

Fill the website with relevant content: useful articles on weight loss

To fill your website with relevant and quality content, you can write articles on weight loss or outsource this work to someone else, if you were not a great writer, I would look at a site like Upwork (payment) to find the talent you have need to get quality content.

Promote your website: SEO, social media, advertising

There are some things you can do to promote your website in the hope of attracting more visitors to your website. For example, while adding content, make sure you're doing at least some basic search engine optimization (SEO). Write quality articles in such a way that search engines believe your site has important information when people enter search words on weight loss.

In addition to SEO, create a page on social networks and promote content. Remember that social media are important for spreading and sharing your pages. (read lesson 18 and 19) You can advertise your site for free on Social Traffic, where you can also directly sponsor your affiliate links and banners.

Avoid being overwhelmed: Take it one step at a time

It's easy to be overwhelmed at the beginning because the whole process is not exactly small, but you'll never have to try doing it all at once. You can take one step at a time, and when you do, you'll find out that it's not that hard.

Affiliate marketing is a real way of building your online business, and with a bit of hard work and time it can lead to a solid online income.

So do not overwhelm you trying to read everything right away. It's too much to take all at once. The most important thing is to do everything calmly, without haste.

6. How to start Affiliate Marketing without a website

Building a website is the most common way for affiliates to launch themselves into the world of affiliate marketing and, if you are interested in creating a long-term business, you will need to create a website.

However, if you're still learning about web design or just are not interested in building a website, there are other ways to sponsor your affiliate links, let's see **how to start Affiliate Marketing without a website**.

Remember: the key to success with affiliate marketing is to get a sale from an interested audience from your affiliate link - how you choose to do it is up to you! Here are some methods you could try:

- **Promote your products through advertising campaigns on Facebook**

Facebook is the most famous and known social network in the world, visited every day by millions of users and if you do a good advertising campaign you will surely have excellent results. Many affiliates use this social network to make profits, and it is an excellent resource that you can use. In addition you have the opportunity to make targeted campaigns by choosing age, or just women, etc. Do not post links on your personal wall or share the link with friends, the results are very poor. I suggest you create an advertising campaign. (read lesson 18)

- **Post on Blog and Forum**

This is a very simple way to get a taste for affiliate marketing: all you need to do is find a product you want to promote, then start posting on blogs and forums with your affiliate link in your signature.

Obviously you have to post only on blogs and forums where people might be interested in the product - you will not get many sales for a weight loss product on a car enthusiast forum.

In the same way, you will discover that you are much more successful if you create useful and interesting posts and if you become a regular forum user. Once this is established, people will begin to respect your opinion and will be more inclined to click on your link. If you simply post on a blog or forum with unnecessary posts, it is very likely that you will be banned and your posts deleted.

All the secrets on how to earn from $20,000 to $100,000 per month with Affiliate Programs

- **Write a viral eBook or some other "viral" product**

A "viral" product is designed to spread (often quickly) to many people - this can be a great way to advertise your affiliate links without having to create a website. You can write a short 30-page eBook on a particular topic, post links to your affiliate products, and then distribute your book through whatever medium you want. You can sell it for a small amount on Amazon or eBay for example.

If your book is informative and useful, rather than simply laden with affiliate ads, you may find that it spreads fairly well.

- **Promote your affiliate links or banners through specific marketing sites**

One of the many sites that I want to recommend is <u>Social Traffic</u>, this site deals with Marketing and you can easily advertise your links or banners, it is great even if you want to advertise your site and your social pages. It is a complete Digital Marketing site.

- **Create a series of videos on YouTube**

YouTube has conquered the world with one billion unique visitors per month. You can use this to your advantage. It does not take much more than a webcam and some bizarre or informative ideas to make a channel work. This way you can add affiliate links in your description or video and convert some of those fans and visitors into profits.

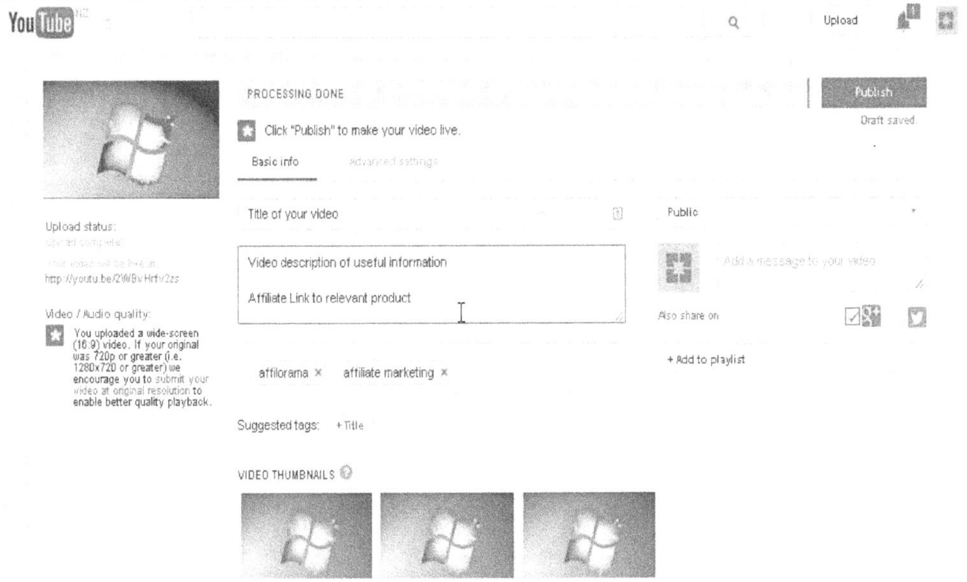

All the secrets on how to earn from $20,000 to $100,000 per month with Affiliate Programs

Choose a niche and create a series of videos related to that topic, with a related affiliate promotion. In this way, viewers you receive will be more likely to be interested in the affiliate product, as they already have some interest in watching your videos.

There are two main rules to do this, however, that you MUST respect:

1. **The content must be full of value for the viewers. Financial gain must be secondary to this.**
   If your video is obviously only there for you to make money from a link, you will be listed as spam, and your efforts will become useless. Producing something useful is much more successful and in this way we get the attention and respect of potential customers.

2. **Do not be misleading!**
   If your video is not related to your link or the title or description claims something that is not in the video, you're violating YouTube policies. This too is something to avoid.

Basically, video marketing on YouTube can be a risk, because affiliate links can be listed as spam, but the best way to avoid it is to be honest and useful. Avoid spam behavior. Some quality content options could include:

- Reviews of honest and informative products
- Educational videos (for example, if your niche was food and nutrition, you could do cooking demonstrations)
- Thematic discussions (eg Tips for keeping food fresh or interesting nutritional data)

Just have a link in the description, and possibly one on the video if it is extremely relevant (like a video review of the product). If you want to be particularly careful, note somewhere that you are an affiliate or that the link is an affiliate link and contact YouTube to clear up right away. If your videos have a value for the viewer and this stands out more than your efforts to make money, this should not be a problem.

- **Promote affiliate products via PPC (Pay Per Click) ads**

I left this method last because, frankly, it's not what I recommend. This method involves creating pay-per-click campaigns through search engines like Google or Bing, promoting the merchant's website directly through your affiliate link.

Herbal Medicines Adelaide
Naturopathy and Homeopathy. Treat
Ailments The Natural Way. Call Now!
HerbalHomeopathicDispensary.com.au

2008's Hair Loss Reviews
Ranking Of The Top Hair Loss
Treatments Currently Available!
www.Hair-Loss-Rankings.com

Hair Loss Product Reviews
Which Ones Really Work? We
List The Top Hair Loss Treatments
www.Hair-Loss-Advisory.com

Leimo Hair Laser On Sale
Proven to REGROW Hair, Money Back
Guarantee, Cheapest prices in Aus!
www.ry.com.au

Hair Transplant Surgeon
Over 30000 Transplants Performed
Winner of The Golden Follicle Award
www.RichardShiell.com.au

So instead of using PPC to promote your own website, you send them straight to the merchant.

There are a number of downsides to this method.

1. First, with Google's AdWords in particular, there will only be one paid listing for a particular website displayed at any given time. This means that instead of competing against other advertisers for one of eight spots on the page, you're competing for just one spot. If you bid a large amount and write an attractive ad then you might see your ad displayed, otherwise you can forget it.

2. Secondly, you have no control over the quality of the merchant page. Increasingly the search engines are looking at the page you're promoting and deciding whether this offers a good experience for their users. If the merchant site has little content, or poor quality content, you could end up paying a much higher amount for your advertisements.

There are always new affiliates who see this as a fast and easy way to get started, but we really recommend that you try the other methods we've introduced first.

7. How to find the products to promote

One of the best places to start when starting Affiliate Marketing is to investigate what affiliate programs you can work with. Now let's see how to find products in affiliation. Let's take a closer look at ClickBank, one of the largest affiliate networks on the Internet and home to some fairly high-end products, and I'll show you other networks to check out.

But first let's start with what is an affiliate network?

Introduction to Affiliation Networks

Affiliate networks are the coordinators of the affiliated world. They coordinate between the merchant and the affiliate, are responsible for the processing of payments by the customer, keep track of affiliate commissions and paying affiliates.

They are a great place to start when you're looking for affiliate products to promote, as many have a directory that you can consult by topic.

Let's take a look now at: **ClickBank**

ClickBank is one of the best affiliate networks for digital products, such as software and eBooks. The good thing about software and eBooks is that they tend to have much higher commissions compared to physical products. (You can probably understand why: software and eBooks have no production costs per item, so traders do not have to worry about affiliate commissions that cut margins.) Fees between 50% and 75% are reasonably common for digital products.

If you click on "Market" you will be directed to the ClickBank affiliate product directory: here you can consult affiliate programs by topic:

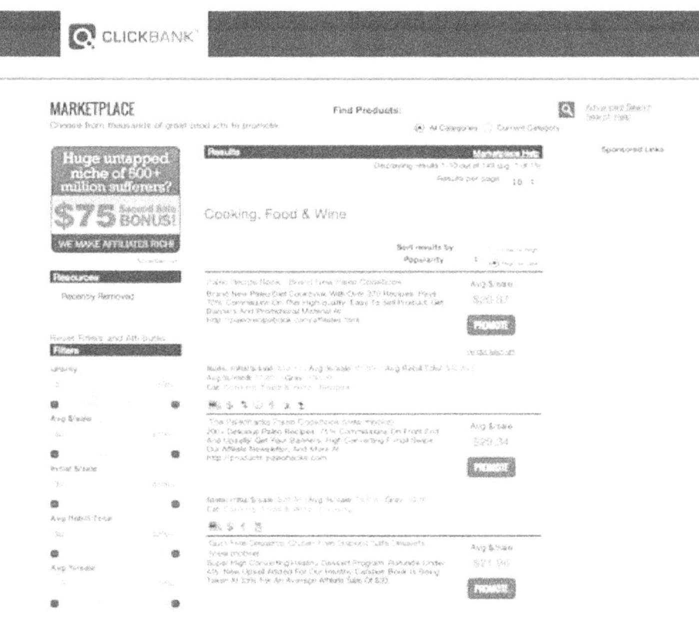

ClickBank provides some statistics on affiliate programs in their listings.

Initial $/sale = How much you earn for each sale

Avg %/sale = What percentage of the sale price makes up your cut.

Avg Rebill Total = If the product has recurring billing (for example, monthly memberships) then this is the amount of money you might you expect beyond the initial sale. If the product doesn't have recurring billing this figure will be blank.

Avg %/Rebill = This number is only shown if the vendor offers products with recurring billing, and shows the average commission rate earned on that part of the income.

Grav = **Gravity** Gives an indication of how hot a product is at the moment. Products with high gravity have a lot of affiliates making money selling this product, while those with low gravity have comparatively less affiliates selling the product. Take this figure with a grain of salt, since it is open to manipulation, but in general you'll probably want to look at products that have a decent amount of affiliate activity, since that obviously means that people are making money from them.

Signing up to become a ClickBank affiliate is a fairly straightforward process: click the "Sign up" link at the top of the page, fill in the details as required, click "Submit" and follow instructions from there.

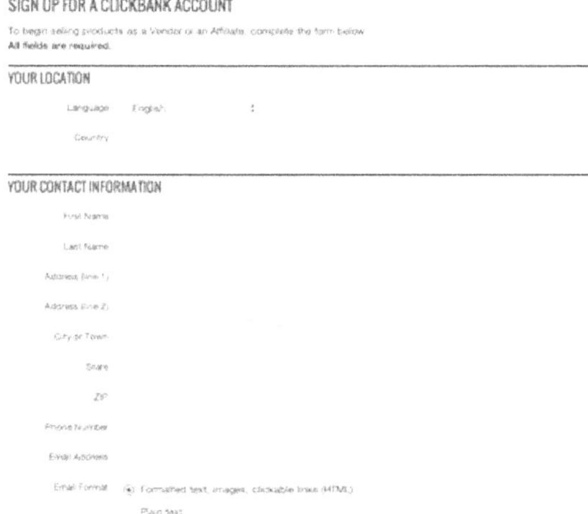

Once you have your ClickBank ID, you are able to promote any product on the ClickBank network. When you browse the products you will see a link to "Promote".

All the secrets on how to earn from $20,000 to $100,000 per month with Affiliate Programs

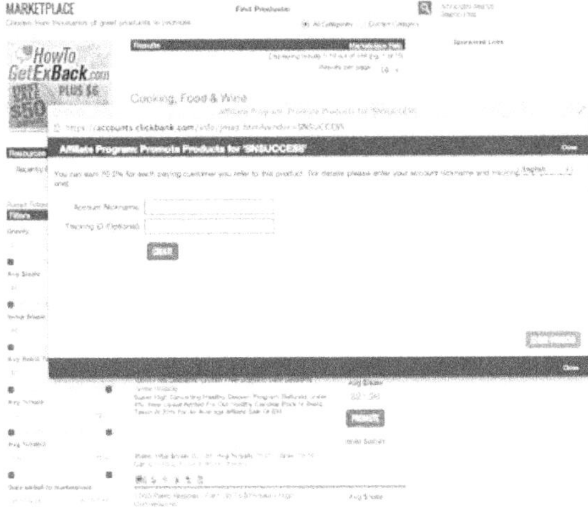

Click "Promote", then click on "Generate HopLinks" (generate affiliate link), it will come out immediately after your link to promote, click on "Copy HopLink" and you can start promoting your product.

You must use the HopLink each time you connect to the merchant's site. If you simply connect to the merchant site using the usual address of the website, you will not receive credit for visitors who click on the link and then buy, as they will not be tracked!

Log in to your ClickBank account

When you belong to an affiliate network, you can check how much you have gained by logging into your account and reviewing your statistics. ClickBank groups the commissions of the entire account into a daily amount, which is displayed on the first page when you log in.

Weekly Sales Snapshot

Week Ending	Gross Sales
Dec 08 (current week)	$1,680.10
Dec 01	$1,765.15
Nov 24	$1,441.39
Nov 17	$1,461.45
Nov 10	$1,585.70

Daily Sales Snapshot

Mon	Dec	06	$152.09
Sun	Dec	05	$196.61
Sat	Dec	04	$344.27
Fri	Dec	03	$259.43
Thu	Dec	02	$448.78
Wed	Dec	01	$278.92
Tue	Nov	30	$254.94
Mon	Nov	29	$316.03
Sun	Nov	28	$188.46
Sat	Nov	27	$192.11
Fri	Nov	26	$173.92
Thu	Nov	25	$456.94
Wed	Nov	24	$182.75
Tue	Nov	23	$67.00
Mon	Nov	22	$184.21

You can also deepen your statistics and break them down by product in the reports section.

This was a basic introduction to ClickBank. However there are many other affiliate networks that you might consider. Other networks you could take a look at are:

Other affiliation networks (deepening lesson 9)

- PayDotCom: https://paydotcom.com

- ShareASale: https://shareasale.com

- Rakuten Marketing: https://rakutenmarketing.com

- ClixGalore: https:www.clixgalore.com

Other ways to find affiliate programs

Some companies operate outside affiliate networks, so you will not see them listed in directories. If you want to promote a particular company or a specific product, I suggest you to search the company or the product on Google and make the affiliation request. Keep in mind that almost all companies have an affiliate program on their site, such as Apple, Nike, Adidas, Samsung, Huawei and many others. Just go to their site and find the **Affiliate Program** item that is usually below.

At this point you just have to register and hope that the application is accepted. Many large companies and known as those mentioned earlier, have a large affiliation request and their selection is much more widespread. But trying does not cost you anything.

8. How to get traffic on your website using alternative methods

Pay Per Click (PPC) and Search Engine Optimization (SEO) are certainly not the only ways to attract visitors to your site. In this lesson I show you **how to get traffic to your website using alternative methods**.

Successful affiliates usually make a point of diversifying their traffic sources: relying too much on any traffic source leaves your business vulnerable to the whims of search engines, or dramatic changes in PPC costs. If you are all alone on PPC and SEO to get traffic to your site, you may be in trouble when the situation becomes sour. Furthermore, by limiting yourself to SEO or PPC methods you could lose a lot of potential traffic. Here are a couple of ways to mix things up a bit:

Links from other sites

Getting links to your site is an extremely important part of being a successful affiliate. Not only do they provide a little traffic to your site regardless of search engines, they also help your search engine rankings.

Although linking is a huge part of search engine optimization, try not to think about links purely in terms of the SEO benefits they offer. You may be able to get links from sites that are below, but that offer a lot of high quality traffic to your site. Always remember that your purpose is to attract visitors to your site and that any link that transmits traffic to you is a success for you, regardless of whether it helps you move search engines.

Publication on forums and blogs

Forums and blogs can be excellent places to promote your website, as long as the promotion remains slim and is part of other useful content you've added to the conversation; if you simply bombard a random forum with your URLs you will be banned. Likewise, if you post unnecessary comments like badly disguised self-promotion, your posts will probably be deleted.

The best method is to find some high traffic blogs and forums in your market and spend some time reading and familiarizing yourself with the discussions. Start responding to posts with helpful comments to gradually build a reputation as a genuine and useful contributor. Once you have established yourself as a valuable member, people will be more interested in seeing what else you have to say on your website or checking the products you would recommend in your signature.

As already mentioned, do not reject forums and blogs simply because a link from them will not help your SEO - remember that it is the traffic you are looking for, and if the traffic comes from these blogs or forums, then this is a successful promotion.

9. Alternatives to ClickBank

I did the research for you and I compiled some information on the best ten alternatives to Clickbank. This way, you can learn everything you need to know about an affiliate network, rather than searching all over the web.

You will learn a bit about how they work and what you can expect, as well as how you compare with Clickbank. At the end there is a summary to make everything easier. Let's start.

1 - Rakuten LinkShare

Rakuten LinkShare offers affiliate programs of big brands, but you have to apply to promote them and it is not always easy to be accepted. Better for those with some experience already.

Rakuten LinkShare is an affiliate network for physical products with a wide range of product options, including some known brands.

The registration process and moving within it is a little more complicated than other networks. That said, they give you some information.

The welcome email you get after signing up provides a lot of useful information on how to get started, and when you connect for the first time, there's a little help with tips.

When you browse the catalog for products to promote, you must apply to be accepted by each advertiser.

This means that you have to wait for approval and meet advertiser standards before you can promote your products. Moreover, due to what marketers are paying for the use of this network, commission rates are lower than other networks.

How Rakuten LinkShare compares with ClickBank

- Clickbank is fast and easy to sign up, while Rakuten LinkShare is much more complicated and elaborate.
- Clickbank acceptance is instantaneous for all products, while it is not guaranteed that you are accepted to promote the products you want with Rakuten LinkShare.
- Unlike Clickbank, LinkShare is a network of physical products.
- There are big brands on LinkShare, much bigger than you could find on Clickbank.
- The downside of this is that the bigger the brand, the less likely you will be approved to promote the product.
- If you are a marketing affiliate with some experience, on LinkShare you may find just what you need.

2 - Affiliate CJ

CJ Affiliate is easy to use and full of useful statistics. There is a great variety of types of products to promote.

With CJ Affiliate, you must apply to be accepted by advertisers. This takes some time compared to the immediate acceptance of many other networks (such as ClickBank).

However, it is usually not too difficult to be accepted by most.

In CJ Affiliate, it is easy to filter product searches based on variables such as category, useful area, language, currency, etc. This makes it very convenient to find the best products to promote quickly.

Once you have identified the types of products you are looking for, you can further refine your options with the information provided. The network has practically everything you might need to know, including:

- Network earnings (greener, better!).
- The average EPC (earnings per click) of the last 3 months.
- The average EPC of the last 7 days.
- How much you will earn from a sale.

Clicking on any product will provide even more information about the company, including a description, program terms and more.

Affiliate CJ has a wide variety of products to promote.

Affiliation CJ compared with Clickbank

- Affiliate CJ has digital products that you can promote as Clickbank, but also has physical products.
- You need to get approval from advertisers, which is not the case with Clickbank, so it's a slower process. However, I did not have too many problems to be accepted.
- There is a lot of information about the products available for comparison, so you can make an informed decision about what to promote: both networks are really suitable for this.

3 - ShareASale

ShareASale is another well-known affiliate network with many product options.

It is simple and easy to subscribe to ShareASale, but it is not the easiest platform for browsing available features.

Search for merchants by placing the mouse over the top merchant icons, then select "Search merchants" from the menu that appears.

Options include keyword search, category or a mixture of information in an advanced search.

You can review information about any affiliate product, such as statistics like this:

All the secrets on how to earn from $20,000 to $100,000 per month with Affiliate Programs

Commission Structure	Cookie	Details
20.00% Per Sale	60 Days	

	EPC	Reversal	Ave. Sale	Ave. Comm
7 Day	$273.27	0.00 %	$92.25	$18.88
30 Day	$246.42	0.00 %	$88.01	$17.91

It is not easy to join affiliate programs. Often you have to ask the dealer to resell his products and you are not always accepted.

A convenient feature that ShareASale has developed is the ability to add products to your "shopping cart", which means you can assemble a collection of merchants or products for which you want to save information, then request them, review them or export that information later.

A wide range of physical and digital products exists on this network.

How ShareASale compares with Clickbank

- It is not so easy to navigate / use the features on ShareASale as on ClickBank.
- ShareASale has physical products and digital products, unlike ClickBank, which mostly has digital products.
- It is easier to save lists of favorite products and / or traders on ShareASale than on Clickbank due to the "cart" system.
- The process of joining affiliate programs is much more involved in ShareASale than in ClickBank, as you often have to prove that you have your own website.

4 – Market Health

Market Health is the best solution for affiliates seeking to promote physical products in health-related niches.

Market Health is an affiliation network with a wide variety of health products. Some of the categories include general health, weight loss, colon health, men's health, cosmetics, health and beauty, skin care, sports nutrition and others.

It is very easy to register and the site is extremely simple to use. You can browse by product category, you can watch their products on display or you can sort by country and language.

All the secrets on how to earn from $20,000 to $100,000 per month with Affiliate Programs

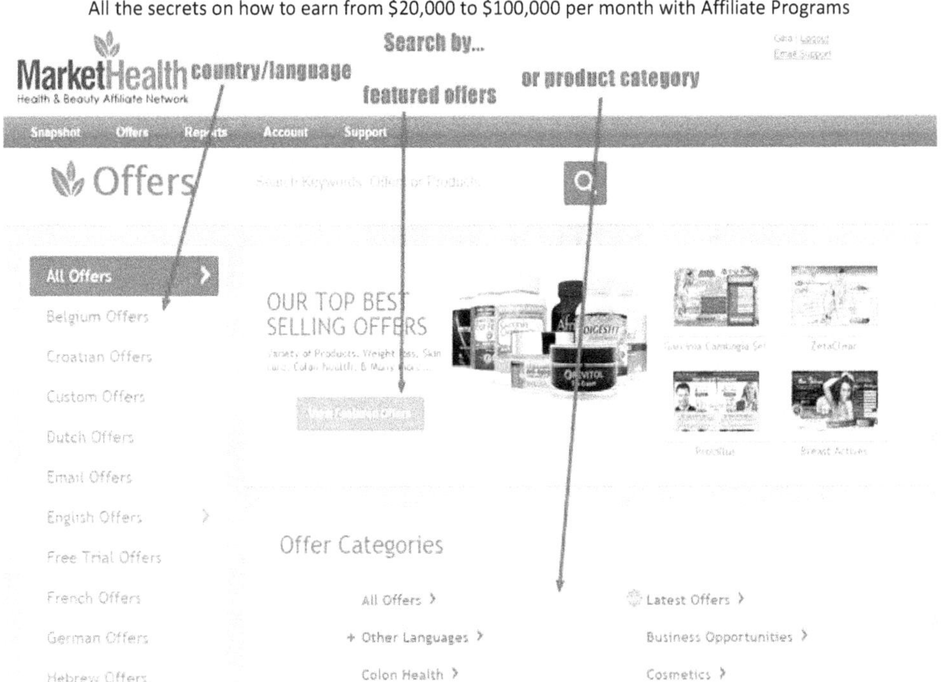

It is therefore possible to examine the variety of products available, each indicating the CPA (cost per action). Clicking on a specific product will open a page containing all the necessary information about it, including payment by conversion, a preview of the sales page and a tracking link.

You can customize your tracking link in a variety of ways, such as generating a version of TinyURL or adding sub IDs so you can examine the performance of specific links in a conversion report.

Some products also have other resources available, such as banners that you can use on your site. All information on this will be found on the product page.

How Market Health compares with Clickbank

- Market Health has a smaller range of products than ClickBank, as it only addresses health-related niches.
- Having said that, if you are in one of those niches, then Market Health is a great specialized resource, much more than Clickbank.
- Clickbank is an affiliation network with predominantly digital products, while Market Health revolves around physical products.
- Clickbank has a gravity filter that helps you select products based on their success rate with other affiliates. Since there is no obvious version for this within Market Health, you're a bit 'darker about the performance of a given product.
- To get around this problem, you can always browse the featured product section if you

want to play it safe, as these have proven to be the best sellers.

5 - Affiliate.com

Affiliate.com tends to prefer middle and advanced affiliates, so if you do not have much experience then you should probably try one of the other networks first. There is not as much information on Affiliate.com as there are for other networks, but what I found was positive.

To subscribe to the site, you must complete an affiliation application, which the site will examine within 2 working days. You will receive a call to confirm all your information and be assigned to an affiliate manager.

Right now, Affiliate.com claims almost 3,000 live campaigns in a variety of categories, so there's definitely a wide selection to choose from.

How Affiliate.com compares with Clickbank

- Affiliate.com offers CPA offers rather than digital products.
- Affiliate.com favors the marketing experts more than Clickbank, which requires no experience.
- The application process for Affiliate.com is more involved and requires to wait for approval.
- Affiliate.com has active affiliate managers, so you're likely to have more contacts with them than Clickbank.

6 - JVZoo

A network of digital products such as Clickbank.

JVZoo is very similar to Clickbank as it is a network of affiliates and vendors based on digital products.

It is easy to navigate and, just like with Clickbank, you can check the market to get an idea of the products you could promote before you signed up.

I have to say that I found some negative reviews that gave me a break, and in looking around I found some gaps.

I chose a random category on the market to get an idea of the products - the general subcategory of the broadest self-improvement category - and I discovered that the first product I clicked brought me to an error page that said that the URL could not be recovered. I also noticed that the same product had a terrible grammar, which did not fill me with confidence:

Essential Aromatherapy

Have you always wanted to know what is aromatherapy? Here are some invaluable information on aromatherapy! Do you ever find yourself unable to cope and get through your day? Do you feel the need to soothe your body and mind from the stresses of modern li

I know this seems a bit fussy, and it is true that many people make money with JVZoo and that some of the products are fine.

Tim says

December 2, 2014 at 5:43 pm

JVZoo's my primary source as I like to promote internet marketing products. I agree there is some junk on there, but after awhile you get good at spotting the worthwhile programs and recognizing names from previous launches with good reputations so you know what's worth your time.

Reply

I think the key to using JVZoo is really to look at what you're promoting before going ahead with it to avoid risking your website's reputation for low quality products. This is true for any network, but it is especially important here.

How JVZoo compares with Clickbank

- Both promote digital products, so it's a very direct comparison.
- JVZoo's online reputation for product quality is a bit poor
- Clickbank has a clearer filtering process (such as gravity filtering) to help affiliates find good products to promote
- They are both easy to explore, free and instant to sign up for.

7 - PeerFly

A high quality CPA network, which prides itself on being custom built.

Peerfly is another CPA affiliate network, again with high quality offers and a great reputation, but you have to apply and be approved.

This verification process is really a good thing. It means that if you are accepted, you are in good hands. Networks that use this type of effort are not easy to register as instant access networks, but because they value integrity and quality. It only means that there is a bit of waiting for the processing of your application.

The nice thing about PeerFly is that the software is custom built, so it is unlikely that downtime or other hosting problems will occur.

You can apply to be a publisher from anywhere in the world. PeerFly has convenient payment options. You can also opt for weekly payments, so you will not have to wait to get your commissions. The site offers PayPal, Payoneer, checks and wire transfers.

You can also access your statistics on your phone via the mobile statistics page.

How PeerFly compares with Clickbank

- PeerFly offers CPA offers rather than digital products.
- The application process for PeerFly requires waiting for approval, which may take some time if there is a backlog of applications. Clickbank is instantaneous.
- They are both very user-friendly.
- PeerFly is smaller than Clickbank, but much more focused on filtering unwanted products and shaded sellers.

8 - Amazon Associates

A huge variety of products to promote, but low commissions.

amazon associates

Everyone has heard of Amazon. It's a great e-commerce and as an affiliate you can take advantage of this huge advantage.

This is probably one of the widest networks you could promote, with something for almost every niche. It is also extremely easy and immediate to start promoting products.

You also get the advantage of Amazon's credibility. People have heard of Amazon, they know it's a legitimate website and are much more confident about buying from it than buying an unknown product from a website.

The main disadvantage of Amazon is that the commissions you can earn here are very small, so you have to have a lot of traffic and make a lot of sales to make a good profit.

You also have a small 24-hour window where your contacts will have to buy in order to make your commission.

It can be difficult to get approval. You need a website, because getting approval without it is highly unlikely. If you do not receive a lot of traffic, you may not be accepted, but without much traffic this network will not give you any benefits.

How Amazon Associates compares with Clickbank

- Amazon has many more products in a large variety of categories compared to Clickbank.
- Amazon has physical products, while Clickbank has mainly digital products.
- Amazon's sales pages have a credibility that other sales pages (like those found through Clickbank) do not have.
- The percentage of Amazon's commissions is much, much lower than that of Clickbank.
- You have to push a lot more sales through Amazon than Clickbank to make a profit.
- You must prove that you have a website to register with Amazon and you must wait for approval, while the process of registering with Clickbank is simple, easy and fast.
- They are both easy and intuitive to understand and use.

9 - eBay Partner Network

Great variety of products, but to be successful you need a website with quality traffic.

eBay Partner Network is a story very similar to the Amazon Associates network. There's a huge amount of products available to promote and you get the added advantage of eBay's credibility: people know that it's safe to buy from eBay.

It's hard to be accepted on this network, unless you have a website with a lot of quality traffic, which is quite fair, since you need quality traffic to earn a decent commission anyway.

How the eBay partner network compares with Clickbank

- The eBay partner network has many more products available to promote than Clickbank.
- EBay Partner Network has physical products unlike Clickbank, which is predominantly digital products.
- eBay sales pages have a credibility that other sales pages (like those found through Clickbank) do not have.
- You must sign up and have a website with high quality traffic to sign up for the eBay partner network.

- You must wait for approval, while the Clickbank sign-up process is simple, easy and fast.
- They are both easy and intuitive to understand and use..

So what should I choose?

Depending on individual marketing needs, you can choose one or more networks to promote from.

If you are looking for digital products, ClickBank is actually one of the best networks. It has high commission rates and a wide range of products to choose from, many of which are of good quality.

If you have not found what you are looking for with Clickbank before, I would try to use the gravity filter to find the best niche and products before giving up. Alternatively, if you're looking for physical products, rather than Clickbank's digital products, the best options are:

- Rakuten LinkShare
- Affiliato CJ
- Market Health

If you have a lot of experience and traffic or a large social following, you could try the Amazon and eBay promotion. It's just about having the right audience to promote products from these well-known sites.

10.   12 essential tips to increase productivity

Many of you will start this business by already having a full-time job, so learning how to get the most out of the few available hours is essential. Sometimes it's even harder to be efficient if you do not have all day to do it, so time management is needed in this case. That's why now we'll look at the **12 essential tips to double your productivity**

1: Use time management software
I recommend ClockingIt.com – it's free.

Add activities in progress and select an expiration date. When you start working on a task, click on the "start work" icon and ClockingIt will start the timer. Click the icon again when you finish working on the activity. You can continue to stop and start until you've finished the task - at which point ClockingIt will tell you how much you've been through.

All the secrets on how to earn from $20,000 to $100,000 per month with Affiliate Programs

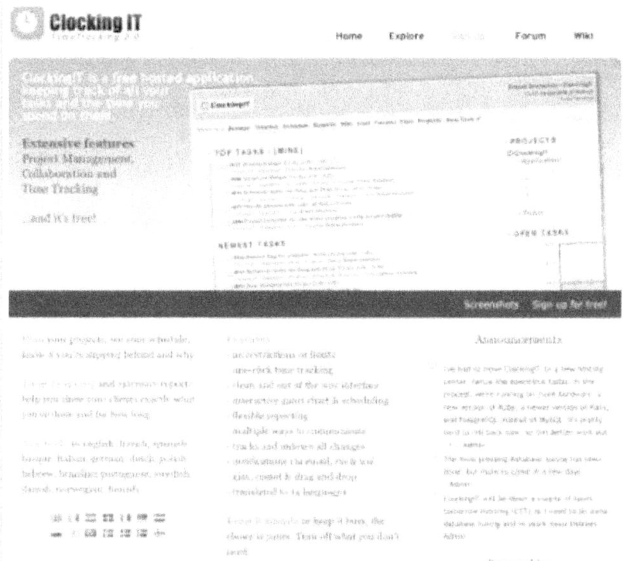

The software makes it easy to see where you're spending your time and spot losses of time (it's pretty shocking to realize that you spent five hours of your work week checking your email!).

You might also find it useful to use a countdown timer for when you want to do a lot of work in a short period of time; try setting the timer for two hours and then working solid for that time, refusing any interruptions. Try doing it a couple of times a day and you'll see great results! (If you're nervous, try 30 minutes to get started). You can still get an incredible amount in 30 minutes if you avoid distractions! Once mastery is acquired, the period of time increases.

2: Keep a notebook of ideas

It's easy to get distracted from anything while you're in the middle of a task. If you follow it, you may inadvertently spend hours of time away from what you really needed to do. Obviously, this is not positive for productivity, but at the same time one does not want to ignore and potentially forget these good ideas.

Dave Allen, author of the amazing book Getting Things Done, recommends to the busy people to keep a 'tickler' file. A 'tickler' file can be a Word document or a notepad. The idea is that a tickler file is a place to quickly enter ideas when you come to mind, so you do not have to stop what you're doing and you can easily find the idea again in the future.

3: Set daily micro goals

Too often we feel overwhelmed by great tasks and end up wandering around doing nothing. The best way to counter this is to make a list of three or five small goals to be achieved each day. You can make your list the night before or the first thing in the morning.

Online activity lists are at your fingertips, but the best thing is actually to pick up a pen and write on paper, so it helps to focus your mind. Setting the micro objectives ensures you get systematically where you want to go. It also helps you feel that you are doing something, every day.

4: Get rid of mess

An ordered office is equal to the ordered mind. If you feel distracted by objects on your desk, chat windows, phone or out-of-window view, simply remove them (or change the desk position). It makes a world of difference for your power of concentration.

5: Limit your email by checking twice a day

Did you know that, for most people, email is the only big break? I advise you to check your e-mail solitaire after noon, as it could be a spam e-mail message that is best left until after you have done an important job. Do not continue to check email all day; Close your e-mail program or your browser window. Focus on your current and limited tasks to accomplish your goals.

6: Learn to say "no"

Being able to succeed over a long period, but this can not be done if you will find yourself constantly interrupted during the day. The solution is to become ruthless: just say "yes" to tasks that can simply be expected, whether they are completed together with the other objectives of the day.

7: Face and finish the worst job first

Procrastination is very distracting. Get into the habit of tackling the task that matters most in the morning, so that your mind does not worry about the rest of the day.

8: Get ideas or things out of e-mail and add them to the list of activities

Going back and forth from the email to check what you need to do can lose precious minutes and increase the likelihood that you overlook something critical. Be sure to immediately add activities from emails to your time management software or a notepad.

9: Use the 80:20 ratio

Eighty percent of your time should be spent on "doing", and no more than twenty percent should be spent on "learning". This is a particularly important lesson for affiliates! We can easily be sucked into sales pitch by Internet marketing gurus, and we all know how long they can be. If you're going to give time to this, or read forums, blogs and newsletters, make sure it fits your schedule to "learn" things - get involved and track how much time you spend, then decide if that time would have been better spent on achieving the goals in your list of activities.

10. Use a mobile phone with a calendar or personal organizer

When you're busy it's easy to forget important appointments. One way to solve this problem is to add appointments and meetings to the mobile phone calendar and schedule the alarm

15 minutes before.

11. Keep a separate to-do list for personal matters

If you suddenly realize that there is something you have to do that has nothing to do with work, write it down in a separate personal to-do list. Keeping your personal life organized ensures that you do not overflow on your business day.

12. Delegate as much as possible

Do not accumulate activities that your staff or family members are more than capable of doing for you. Also, make sure you have set times every day for your work and your personal tasks. This is essential if you want to avoid constant interruptions during the day.

So there are 12 tips to double your productivity! It's easy to downplay or postpone the organization of your business, but setting up efficient business practices is just as important as good SEO or pay per click strategies, so make sure you take them seriously!

11.   What is the fastest way to get started online

Once you've decided to start as an affiliate, there are two ways you can choose to build your business:

1. **Slow and steady,** with minimal additional costs (this is the best method)
2. **Faster, but with additional costs** (but these costs are easy to recover once you're up and running)

Which method you choose depends on how much money and time you can spend and how fast you need to see the results.

For all those who want to see the results FAST and ready to spend some money to make the ball spin faster, this is my simplest and most direct method.

Step 1: Create a website of a page

I see many newcomers get bogged down with the creation of great websites with lots of content: not only is it necessary to create all of this content, but it is also necessary to understand how to put together your website.

So instead of creating all those extra content, you just have to create a one page website.
The only thing you will have on your site is a page that tells people to subscribe to your newsletter. We call this type of page as a "squeeze page".

All the secrets on how to earn from $20,000 to $100,000 per month with Affiliate Programs

In practice, a page very similar to this, with only two options: SUBSCRIBE.

Step 2: Give them a good reason to sign up

To encourage people to subscribe to your newsletter, offer them an incentive on your squeeze page, like a free book, a podcast, an exclusive video, etc. (as in picture)

The work of your squeeze page is to make people really want it. So you have to make it irresistible. Tell them all the excellent things they are about to learn. Tell them how it will help them. Build their curiosity with mysterious points such as:

• Discover the best X things you should never do when XYZ

• The 7 steps for ABC ... you do not need XYZ!

Add an enticing image of your incentive: if it's a book, turn it into an image of a book in 3D so that it looks more precious.

You can easily find someone who can help you on this by going to Fiverr and try searching for "3D book cover" (payment)

You can also say that it is on special offer "normally sold for $ 47" (or some other figure in dollars or euros) to give it more value. You make people feel like they're getting something really incredible, special, so they get more results.

Step 3: Link your page to an autoresponder

An autoresponder is an automatic email service. When someone arrives at your page and enters his e-mail address to receive your book / bait, the autoresponder is what captures their e-mail address, and automatically sends them the things that have been promised.

To make it work on your website you need to register on a site that does this work like Fluttermail, AWeber, GetResponse or others that you can easily find on the web. They'll give you a snippet of code to add to your website that will do all the hard work.

Step 4: Add pre-set e-mails to your autoresponder

Your autoresponder can also drip emails to your subscribers at regular intervals: preload them into your autoresponder, and every time a new subscriber joins, they will start right at the beginning of the sequence.

You can use this to automatically send emails that promote affiliate products. When one of your subscribers clicks on a link in your email and purchases one of the affiliated products ... you will receive the commission.

The longer your subscriber stays subscribed to your newsletter, the more chances they will have to buy something and the more valuable it will be. So find the right balance between giving them enough information to make them happy and make sales.

A warning: this system is based on the fact that your subscribers are growing and start to trust you and your opinion. These e-mails should be well written and they should do a great job by encouraging people to look at your products and buy them.

When your newsletters are set up correctly, they will automatically send emails to your subscribers, automatically making sales for you. And since you already have your squeeze page and "come out" that encourages people to sign up, all you have to do is get visitors to your page to start getting subscribers and making sales!

Step 5: Get visitors to your page (the fastest way)

Here the part "you have to spend money to make money" comes into play.

You need a quick traffic injection so you can start making money. The easiest way to do this is to access other websites that already have a large list of subscribers, and pay them to send an e-mail that promotes your website and your book / bait.

This is called a "solitary ad".

There are directories of websites that sell solitary advertising space, but the most effective way to do this is to look for websites that might be interested in doing it for you.

In fact some of the best sites may not even know what a "solo ad" is. (These can be good because their subscribers have not already been exposed to hundreds of other offers and could be more responsive.)

If you're not looking at a solo ad directory, here's what to look for "in the wild":

• Websites that have a newsletter list: almost all sites have an entry form somewhere on their website.

• Web sites where you can contact the site owner: search for an email address or contact form that you can use to send them a message.

• Websites that attract the kind of people you are trying to attract: if you are a weight loss website, you only need to find a website that has a large audience of women. Easy. If you are a "dating" site, you must find a website that attracts a lot of men. You do not need to be exactly the same topic as your website.

Contact the website and ask if they do sponsored e-mails. Once you have set this up with your advertising provider, the next two steps will take place quickly and automatically.

Step 6: Receive subscribers

A personal ad provider sends an email to your list and some of your subscribers will click through to visit your website and sign up for your book. Boom! You have subscribers.

Step 7: Receive commissions

When these subscribers subscribe to your list, they will start receiving your drip-fed promotional emails. Now you will start to see and receive the commissions.

It may take some time to recover the money spent on the solo ad, but because subscribers tend to stay registered for a long time, you have many opportunities to earn money from them.

Step 8: Take advantage of your list to earn GREAT commissions

The best thing is: once you have a reasonably sized list, you can start earning a lot of money from product launches and promotions. There is always a lot of interest around new product launches, many special discounts and lots of money that must be made by affiliates.

You can email to your list telling them about a new product being launched or a new promotion in progress and you will earn commissions for anyone you buy. This is the way most big marketers make their commissions really big. In some niches it is not uncommon for an affiliate with a particularly large and responsive list of members to make 6 figures over the course of a weekend.

Can you imagine making 6 figures on a weekend? This is only possible if you have a good list of members.

- **Why is it a great way to get started?**
- **You do not need to build a large website**: you only need one page. This cuts a lot of work for a beginner.
- **You do not have to worry about creating many articles**. You only need to create the content for e-mails.
- **You do not have to worry about searching for keywords or creating links to your site**. You do not have to wait for Google to notice it and start improving search engine rankings. When you pay for your visitors, skip this whole passage.
- **All you have to do is get someone to subscribe to your newsletter**, and the newsletter automatically sells for you and you just have to worry about the promotion of the page.

Summary: what you need for this system to work:

- A 1 page "squeeze page" website (web hosting, a domain name and the actual page set on your website)
- Some "bait" to encourage people to register
- Text / images / titles for your squeeze page that "sell" your book for free (ie, they really want people)
- A subscription to the automatic answering service: Eg, Fluttermail, AWeber, GetResponse, or others easily available.
- Email for your automatic response sequence - at least for 30 days (10-15 emails).
- An ad provider that sends email to their list of users to promote your website.

12.   Keyword research: SEO competition analysis

When it comes to doing market research, competition is usually your friend: it means there is money to be made in a market. However, when it comes to optimizing your site for search engines, it's a slightly different story: you need to be able to take a look at the competition out there and decide how good the chances are of classifying well for that word key.

In this lesson, we'll take a look at the SEO **competition analysis** to see if optimization for a specific keyword is worth your time.

How many results?

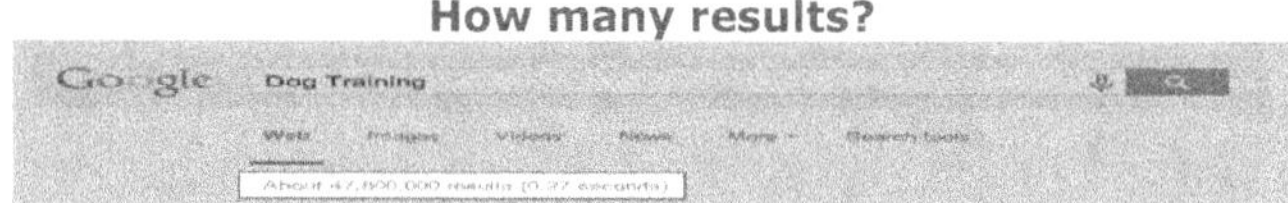

The first (and, too often unique) trick that most affiliates try is to enter their keyword in the search engine to see how many results they get. Unfortunately, when many receive their 12,000,000 results, they become discouraged, abandon that keyword and look for easier collections.

However, it may surprise you that this figure does not mean much and you should take it with a pinch of salt. The "number of search results" is an estimated figure and not all 12,000,000 ads are actually displayed in search results. Also, most of these sites have not performed any search engine optimization, so it's easy enough to beat them.

Rather, use this figure more as an indicator of the presence of activity in the market: if it is super-low (for example, less than a million) it could indicate a lack of interest in that particular word - try to insert it in the word search volume key tool to see how many people are looking for us and see if it confirms this theory.

allintitle:

The next two phases try to identify how well the search engine is optimized. Is it a stroke of luck that classifies well? Or have they designed their sites this way?

One of the key factors of SEO on the page is the text of your title. This is the text that appears between the <title> tags in your HTML code, at the top of the page in your browser, and is the clickable text that appears with your search engine. If a page has a keyword in the title tag, it usually means that they are quite focused on this keyword and have perhaps had some ongoing SEO.

If you enter allintitle: "your keyword" in Google, it will tell you how many sites have your keywords in the title tag. A lower figure is obviously better; anything up to 5000 means you could be there quite easily, but do not discard the keywords just because you get more than 5,000 results in this test. As you will soon see, there are still other factors to consider.

allinanchor:

It is similar to the Allintitle tool, but it indicates how many sites have incoming links with those keywords in the anchor text. Anchoring text is very important for determining your rankings. If there are many sites with your keyword in their anchor text, it makes it harder to classify yourself well. Ideally, you want to see a low number here, but what constitutes "low" depends on the topic and the market. You may need to dig for a while to get an idea of what "low" is.

A technical note for using "allintitle" and "allinanchor" in Google

The quotes on both sides of your keyword are very important for finding the exact keyword phrase in the titles and anchor text. Without the signs of speech, search results could contain words in any order.

For example, during the search: allintitle: "how to cook", the results show the titles with those exact words in that exact order.If there are no quotation marks, the sentence could be subdivided or in the wrong order

Furthermore, the all-in part of allintitle or allinanchor is very literal. You can search for "intitle" or "inanchor." But there is no guarantee that all words will be displayed in the search. You can only do this if you are looking for a series of single words instead of a complete sentence.

To be sure every time you look for competition on certain keyword phrases, use the speech signs around the keyword. This will always return results with the exact phrase, regardless of whether you are using allintitle, allinanchor, intitle or inanchor.

Review the domains:

Another thing to check is the age of your competitors' domains, using the <u>WHOIS</u> tool to check their creation date. Older domains tend to do better in search engines than newer ones, so on the contrary, if most of your competitors have fairly new domains they may be easier to beat.

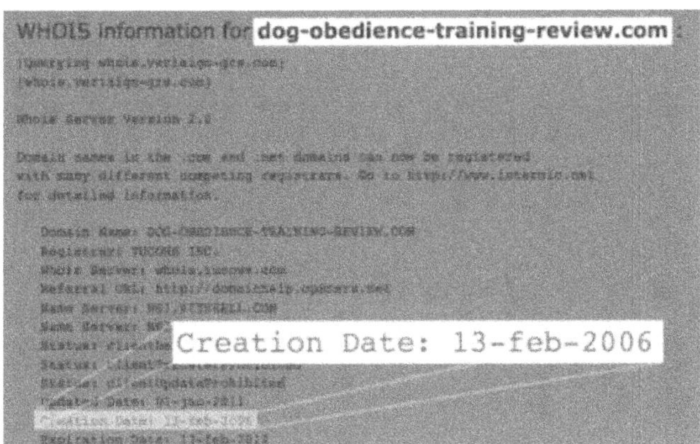

Keep an eye on research volumes:

While doing all these researches, keep in mind another key factor: if someone is actually looking for your keyword!

It is usually the case that the competition overheats when there are many people looking for that keyword, but it is not always equally balanced. Calculate if the number of visitors you will receive from a good ranking is really worth getting this placement: some keywords have too much competition and insufficient traffic to justify the great effort.

Another important consideration when choosing a keyword is if there is actually money in the market! If you find a keyword that seems easy to classify, ask yourself if there's a reason for it. Is it unknown or unprofitable? A good indicator is if there are Google ads on the right side of search engine results - if people pay to get traffic to their sites, then there must be money to be made.

Many keywords to work with?

When building an affiliate site for SEO, you should not focus on a keyword, but you have some - so your main keyword is not the main goal of your SEO campaign.

When looking for markets and keywords, try to find those that have a number of highly sought-after keywords to target. You can use search tools for keywords like Google Trends or Wordtracker to get ideas on search volumes for related keywords.

Search for related keywords

Because these keyword tools typically use the words you enter as a basis for their suggestions, you can often lose the search for related keywords, but not based on the same word. For example, if you were concentrating on "dog training" you could lose a key word like "stop the German shepherd aggression".

A cheap and unpleasant trick you can use to find semantically related words is to enter your keyword in Google with a tilde (~) in front of you. For example, for "garbage can" you can enter:

~ garbage can

When Google returns results, you'll see that there are a lot of words on the page listed in bold. These are related words. "~ garbage can", for example, gets additional words like "waste", "recycle", "containers" and "recycle cans".

Going down the road

If your main keywords seem intimidating, do not completely exclude your chances of success in a market. Take another look (and do some lateral reflection) and see if there are easier words on the market that you can face first. For example, a keyword like "trash cans" has much more competition and would be more difficult to classify.

If you can optimize your site with a few simpler keywords, you can get as much traffic as you rank highly for that difficult keyword. As a bonus, the most targeted search terms tend to earn even more money! A key word like "stopping the German shepherd's assault" is not only easier to classify than "dog training", but people who seek this term are more likely to buy than those who are looking for the more general " dog training ". Maybe it's because they already know what kind of solution they want, or perhaps because you're more able to target your site to their specific interests. Regardless of this, it is a win-win situation for you as an affiliate!

13.   4 steps to find profitable affiliate niches

In this lesson you will learn how to find a profitable affiliate niche. Again, "niche" means "general theme" of the products you will promote as a marketing affiliate. So, if you promote products like "Dating Guides" on a dating site, you'll be in the Encounters' niche.

All the secrets on how to earn from $20,000 to $100,000 per month with Affiliate Programs

The goal: to find a niche that will constantly make money

You can not choose a niche just because you like it. Do not get me wrong, enjoying your niche is a very good thing, but you also need to know that it will make you earn money. Are we here for this or not?

The last thing you want is to spend a lot of time and effort to build an affiliate site just to find out that there are not many profitable products you can promote.

Here's where you need to start: find a niche already full of profitable products, so you know you can make money there.

How to find profitable niches in ClickBank

The most profitable products to promote as affiliates are usually digital offers, such as e-books or online training programs; They often allow you to earn 50-75 percent of the sale, which you could not do with physical products like clothes or toys.

That's why we'll look for profitable niches in ClickBank: it's one of the biggest affiliate networks full of digital products, it's easy to navigate and you can use the "gravity" filter to see which ones sell well and which do not.

You can look at all the products of the platform if you want, but for now we are just trying to see what topics have a good spread of products that sell.

Step 1: Check the categories in the ClickBank Marketplace

When you get to the ClickBank market, you will see that there are a lot of large categories listed on the left.

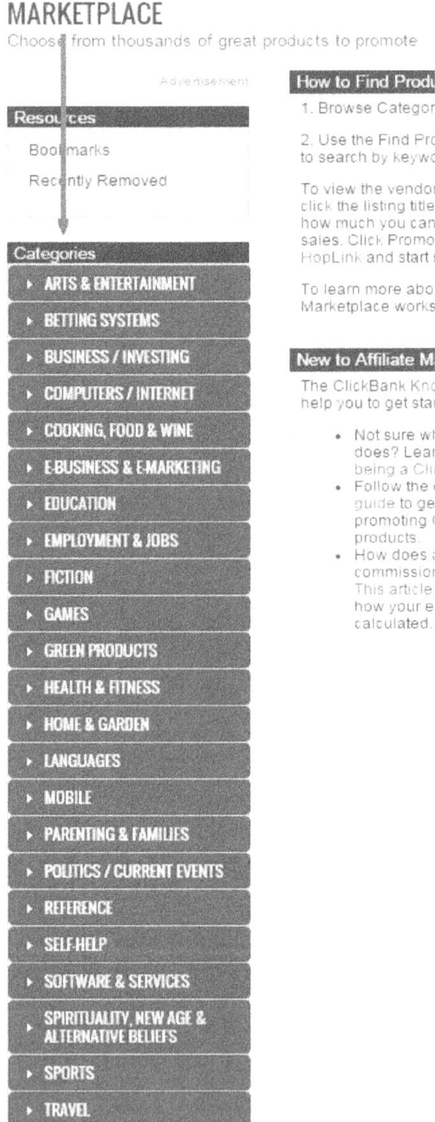

If you click on one of these categories, you'll see even more subcategories to browse. Since there are so many options, it's worth starting out with something that looks interesting. After all, the more you are interested in a subject, the more naturally you will be motivated to do the job.

For my example, I will look at "Dieting and weight loss" in the "Health and Wellness" niche.

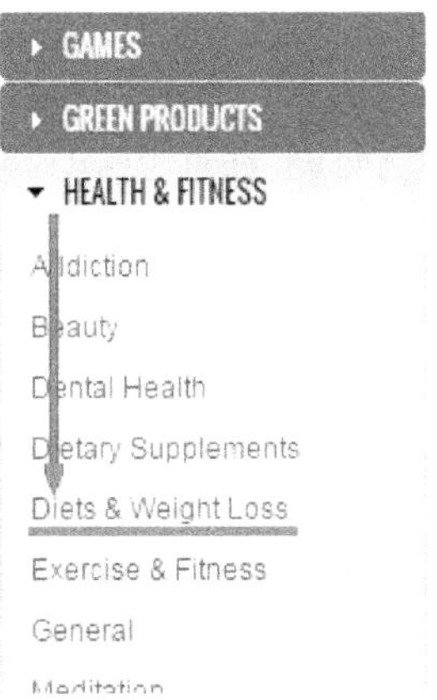

Step 2: Filter products that are not sold
At the moment, I can see 396 products in the "Diets and weight loss" sub-category:

They are so many products! And not everyone will be profitable sellers, so it's time to "cut" the superfluous. Set the minimum severity to 6 to remove products that are not selling well.

All the secrets on how to earn from $20,000 to $100,000 per month with Affiliate Programs

Immediately, this cut 333 products that are not selling. I stayed with 63 profitable products in this subcategory.

Some categories will have many products with a severity of 6 or more, and some will not have them at all. So if the niche you are looking at has no options, after applying the gravity filter, keep looking around.

Step 3: Browse the site to find the best niche options

From here, you can search through the market to find a topic that has a decent number of products with a severity of 6 or more.

This is not always as simple as going through the subcategories in ClickBank. For example, you may find that there are several "detox" -related products, but they are scattered in a couple of different categories.

So you will probably spend some time digging through the categories and looking for topics that appear fairly regularly. A good way to find similar products that could be hiding in different categories is to use the top search box.

For example, if I see "Diets and weight loss", I find a product to burn fat "detox".

I could enter "detox" in the search to see how many other products like this are there with a severity of 6 or more. In this case, there are 23.

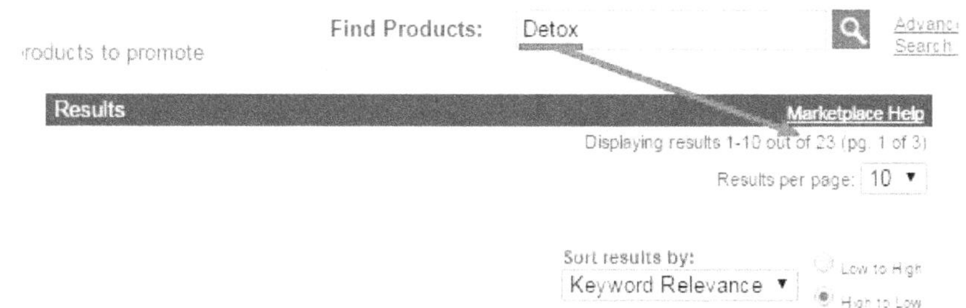

That's why it's a good idea to use the search: I may not have found all these products looking for a category or sub-category. I can think of some sub-categories in which the detox products might be present, but the research allows me to see them all at once.

At this point, I think "detox" looks like a promising niche because it has many products that are already selling well. It's clearly a niche that people are buying.

If you do a search and there are fewer than 10 products with 6+ gravity, it might be better to go and look for something else. This does not mean that with that niche it would be impossible to make money, it could be more difficult than a niche with a lot of products that are selling well.

Step 4: Dig a little deeper; Look at the sales pages

Yup! The detox niche is fine! "I want to see the sales pages of these products to make sure I understand correctly what the niche topic is and that most products are on the subject.

The main product in my research, for example, is a "computer detox" product, which does not fit at all with my original idea of a detox diet:

Fortunately, however, on the first page of my research I can see at least 7 products that are relevant to the niche of detox diet that I had anticipated, like this:

Many of them seem quite professional, and I know they are selling pretty well, so at this point I would feel confident enough to get on with the detox niche.

It may take some time to find what you are looking for

Not all the niche research will be as quick and simple as my example, which was mostly a case.

You might come across some dead ends before discovering a great niche idea. Do not be discouraged! Make yourself a cup of tea, coffee or hot chocolate and take some time to look around and reflect.

The search for the right product is **essential**, do not be in a hurry.

Other things to consider before settling in a niche

If you've done the research above and you've made your decision based on the data, chances are you've found a good niche. However, there are some extra things you may want to consider before making a decision:

A) This niche is "Evergreen"?

It is important to think about the business: "Will these types of products always be popular?"

Also, some products could be sold well now, but their popularity could be seasonal. For example, the niche of the "costume trial" will only work during the months prior to summer.

To make sure that affiliate marketing is worthwhile, you need to look for something that will be profitable throughout the year, for many years to come.

Usually you can make a logic based hypothesis, but here we are going to **make money**, never forget it. If you want to be sure, try Google Trends. For example, if I enter "detox" and set it to show the results of the last 12 months, I can see that he had a constant interest throughout the year with a peak in January (probably due to Christmas holiday bingeing).

All the secrets on how to earn from $20,000 to $100,000 per month with Affiliate Programs

If I change my research to show myself in recent years (since 2004), I can see that interest has grown constantly, which is also a great sign.

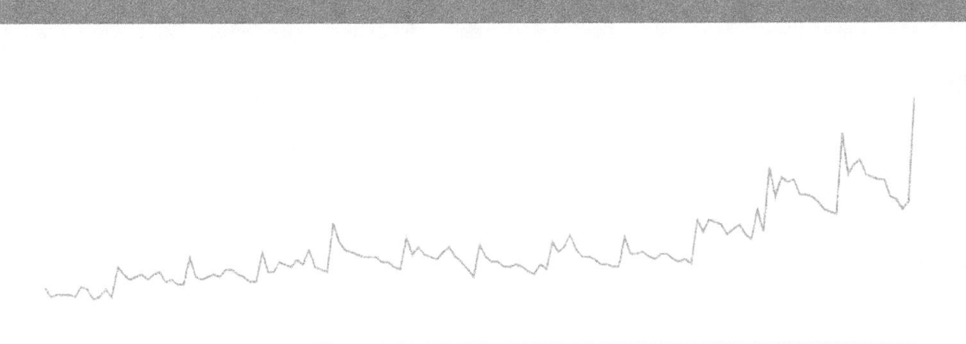

B) Are people looking for this topic in search engines?

Another thing you may want to consider before settling on a niche is: how many people are looking for this topic on Google?

It's great if a lot of people are looking for your niche topic on Google for a couple of reasons: it shows that the niche is in great demand and where there is demand for money. Another important thing is that it will be easier to use SEO (search engine optimization) to get traffic to your website after creating it.

To deepen your search, besides Google Trends you can also use Google Ads to see how many times that word is searched on Google.

If you can find at least 10 phrases or words with at least 1,000 searches per month, then consider that there is a strong interest in the niche and you will be able to use SEO along the way to get traffic to your site.

C) Do you like this niche?

One last thing to consider before settling into a niche is: do you like it? I know that I said before that enjoying a niche is not enough - it must also be above all profitable - and it's true. But it's always easier if you do it with passion and pleasure.

Having at least a little interest in your niche will also make it easier for you to understand your future audience, which will be useful when you're trying to market your site and products.

So, if you're looking for a niche that came to your mind, but you do not really like it, try searching again to see if there's anything that's more interesting to you. The market is vast and you will surely find something, do everything calmly.

At this point you should have a general niche topic, such as "detox" or "puppy training", with a handful of relevant ClickBank products that have a severity score of 6 or more.

If you do not have the above, you need to go back through this lesson, choosing a different niche and products. I can not stress enough how important it is that you correctly complete the niche search process!

If there is one that you like a lot more than others, choose that one. If you love puppies, for example, but the thought of another niche makes you sick - go for the puppy's niche.

The closer your affinity with the niche is, the greater the chance of success.

If you like them all the same or you can not decide yet, look at the one with most products with a severity of 6 or more in ClickBank. So if "diets" have more affiliate products than "puppies training" and you feel at the same level of enthusiasm, choose "detox diets". This approach gives you more shots in promoting profitable products.

14.   How to choose an affiliate program

Before throwing yourself headlong into the marketing activities that will dominate most of your time as an affiliate, it is essential to select a good market in which to exercise your marketing skills. Not all products with affiliate programs are profitable and even the best marketing efforts can be wasted if the program is not attractive to visitors, or does not pay a good commission.

While it is possible to find a profitable market first and then identify affiliate programs within that market, it is actually much faster to do it the other way around. In this lesson, we will discuss **how to choose an affiliate program**.

Step 1: Find a suitable program

ClickBank contains many excellent affiliate programs for digital download products. In general, there are three things that distinguish a profitable program from a waste of precious time.

1. Commission equal to 60% or more

Over the years, I have come to the conclusion that it is not worth the time and effort to promote a product unless the commission is at least 60%. Since most of the ClickBank products retail $ 30 - $ 70, they comply with this rule meaning that you earn a minimum of $ 18 per sale. There are dozens of products in ClickBank that pay 60% or more - the best is 75%.

However, there are a couple of exceptions:

a) Very high selling price: if the product sells for $ 155, then a 50% commission is not so bad and still worth it. Even so, I do not suggest going under a 50% commission.

b) Recurring billing: ClickBank subscription-based products often allow you to continue earning a commission every time the customer pays their subscription. In this case, you can reduce the base to 40%.

2. A high-severity assessment

ClickBank's severity rating is based on the number of different affiliates who made a sale during the week. A high severity rating means that many affiliates are making sales and, in general, you can take this to indicate that the product is in high demand and is likely to be profitable for you.

There is an exception to this rule: Internet marketing products.

Internet marketing products are often purchased by affiliates through their affiliate link. In this way they get a big discount on a product; unfortunately, it also drastically reduces gravity, so when you look at the severity of internet marketing products, do not take the gravity of this type of product at face value. The category that most likely will be affected by this type of activity is Marketing and Ads.

3. Check the sales page

Of course, low gravity is not necessarily unprofitable - after all, every new product must also start at 0! However, if a product has a low gravity, it is necessary to dig a little to understand if it will convert well.

The best way to learn more is to click on the sales page and:

- Check the long sales page. The short page does not tend to convert well.
- Compare the page with competing products. Is it convincing? If competitors have a better looking and better sounding sales page, then there is probably a reason why this product is not doing well.

Example of a good affiliate program

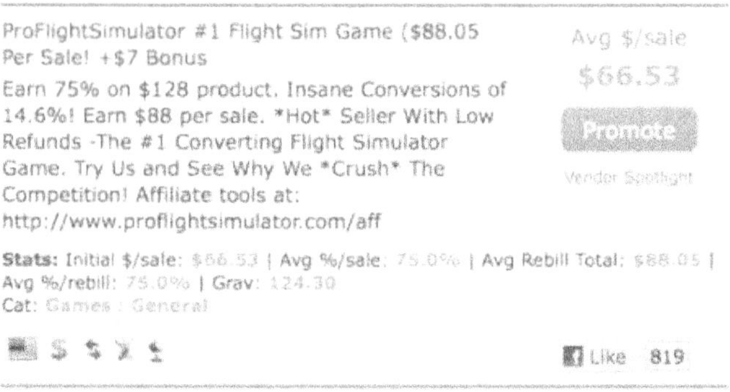

ProFlightSimulator #1 Flight Sim Game ($88.05 Per Sale! +$7 Bonus

Earn 75% on $128 product. Insane Conversions of 14.6%! Earn $88 per sale. *Hot* Seller With Low Refunds -The #1 Converting Flight Simulator Game. Try Us and See Why We *Crush* The Competition! Affiliate tools at: http://www.proflightsimulator.com/aff

Avg $/sale
$66.53

Promote

Vender Spotlight

Stats: Initial $/sale: $66.53 | Avg %/sale: 75.0% | Avg Rebill Total: $88.05 | Avg %/rebill: 75.0% | Grav: 124.30
Cat: Games : General

Like 819

This program, for example, has everything: great gravity, a 75% commission and a high selling price.

Example of an incorrect affiliate program

Easy Face Painting
Step-By-Step Guide Makes Face Painting So Easy Even Non-Creative Types Can Paint Like Pros.

Avg $/sale
$13.22

Promote

Stats: Initial $/sale: $13.22 | Avg %/sale: 50.0% | Grav: 2.15
Cat: Home & Garden : Crafts & Hobbies

Like 42

On the contrary, this product has a very low severity, a low commission and a low selling price; if you were to view the sales page you would also see that it is rather short and not so convincing.

CPA programs

Cost-per-acquisition programs pay a fee for each action, rather than each sale. For example, some CPA programs pay a commission for each captured e-mail address, others for a zip code, and others for completing an application form.

Good CPA programs are:

1. **Postal code offers**. Why? Because they are easy. All you have to do is give a zip code and earn a commission. I know many people who earn over a million dollars a year from CPA bids on the postcode only.

2. **Commissions over $1**. Why? Because earning $ 1 in a sale makes your effort worthwhile. Of course, there are many programs that pay 0.20 per acquisition, but is it worth it?

3. **Unlimited promotion** This is not really a "rule" as such, but more a warning. Some programs seem fantastic in every sense ... but they only allow you to promote them via email. This is fine if you have a list, but what if you do not have it? So make sure you check the terms and conditions before going ahead. You will find that some programs have no restrictions, others have few restrictions and others have many!

Programs of physical products

There is only one rule to choose a good physical product to promote:

Make sure you earn at least $ 40 per sale.
Physical products have a low margin compared to digital products like those offered by ClickBank, so instead of applying the "60 or more commission%" rule, look for at least $ 40 per sale. This means that for a $ 2,500 TV retail, you would want to earn a 2% ($ 50) commission on each sale.

Step 2: Evaluate the market

Now that you've found some affiliate programs that seem likely, it's time to find out how the market is.

A lot of competing affiliates = healthy market

As the saying goes: there is nothing wrong with a bit of healthy competition.

Ideally, an Internet search in the main search term for your market should reveal strong competition from affiliates in the form of many PPC ads. You can take this as a sign that there is money to be made in the market.

For example, a search on "dog training" - a market that we know to be highly profitable - reveals dozens of PPC ads and many are clearly affiliated.

On the other hand, a search on "face painting" only makes five ads appear - and only one of these seems to be an affiliate. This suggests that the face painting market is either uncovered, or unprofitable - almost certainly the latter!

Lots of niche search terms

Competition in primary terms is good, but there still needs to be room to make a profit.

Using the free WordTracker (or a similar tool), your next step is to check the number of niche search terms for the market.

A good market has a lot of niche search terms with relatively little competition - for example, the game 'World of Warcraft' is very popular all over the world. It's a market with many affiliates, but there are also literally hundreds of niche search terms:

All the secrets on how to earn from $20,000 to $100,000 per month with Affiliate Programs

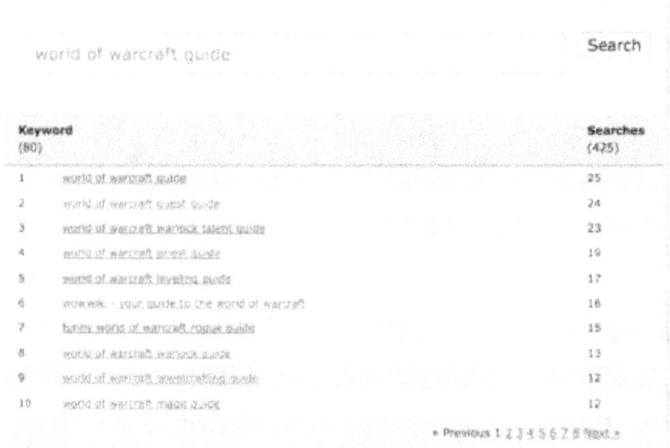

Likewise, competition is intense in the dog training market for that key phrase, but there are many niche terms with low competition such as: 'stop pitbull aggression'

It's not just PPC ads - for example, even if the "stop fox terrier" niche term has a number of competing PPC ads, there seems to be plenty of opportunities for an SEO site for this search term.

Are there more products to promote on the market?

While not strictly necessary, it can be useful if there are several quality affiliate programs within the market that you can promote, especially if you want to create a list.

In a market with multiple affiliate programs, such as the dating market, you could promote "How to attract the opposite sex" for two weeks and then switch to "How to gain self-confidence". A few weeks later you could offer "How to start conversations"; you are offering great value to your list and also continuing to earn money through repeated purchases.

Summary of the lesson

In this lesson we tried to choose a suitable affiliate program and some of the pitfalls to keep an eye on; we have also examined the evaluation of the affiliate market:

Some of the things to keep an eye on when choosing a program include:

ClickBank

- Products should have a commission of more than 50%, preferably over 60% (with some exceptions)
- Check that the product has a high degree of gravity or (if it is a new product) check for a decent sales page

CPA Programs

- Commissions should exceed $ 1
- Pay attention to promotion restrictions (unless these restrictions work to your

advantage)

Physical products

- Look for commissions over $ 40. The second step is the evaluation of the market

- Try to see if the market has healthy competition (it's a good thing), but still has room to grow

- See if there are more quality products to promote in the market

15.   What the market wants

Knowing who your market is and what your market wants is essential to promote or successfully attract people to your site; in this lesson we will study **what your market wants?**

No market research is complete until you have taken a good look at the people and the problems that make up your market. Careful research into the "people side" of your market can help you in many ways:

- You may discover keywords that were not immediately apparent when you only looked at keyword search volumes

- You can determine what your market thinks, aim better and improve your results!

Each market has common concerns and recurring themes, problems and problems for which people need answers - things that drive them to the Internet for information; the role of internet marketers is to find out what these things are and to provide solutions.

Find what people need

As a marketer you can make a plausible hypothesis about the concerns of your market but, unless you already know a lot about your market, the only way to really get into your audience's head is to enter and see what your market is. he's talking.

The first place most affiliates watch is in search volumes for relevant keywords. If, for example, you were thinking about creating a site on chicken recipes, you should link "chicken recipe" to your favorite keyword search tool or search engine and see what kind of keywords with the word "chicken" the most people are looking for.

Forum: The most personal approach

Although keyword volumes are a great way to get a general view of the market, the real strength of market research comes from being able to speak directly and specifically to your client's problems.

Online forums are a good source to take a closer look at your market. The forums give you the opportunity to view and discuss, get a good feeling, for the relevant topics and concerns of your market; they can also give you ideas for related topics for articles and marketing angles you have not thought about.

To find the forums just type in your topic and "forum" in Google. Before you immerse yourself completely make sure you take a quick look to see if there are many people talking and if the forum is well organized; if not, move on to the next one.

Once you've found a suitable forum, even looking at the forum index page you can get good ideas for topics for your website, just like we did in Google.

Digging deeper

At this point you may have noticed good ideas from the general categories of the forum, dig a little 'in the argument to see what they are really talking about people; find out what kind of questions they ask: if you know what your market is asking for, you will be able to respond (or at least recognize) their concerns on your website.

Remember, though, if you take these new ideas and go back to your keyword search tool, you might be a little disappointed with the search volumes. You have to decide for yourself whether or not it is worth pursuing that route, but remember that the most targeted search terms tend to convert much better than more general search terms and it is easier to classify them in search engines.

Demography

"Demography" is a scandalous word, but if you really want your audience to listen to you, you should pay attention to who they really are. Research can get some of this information, but many could be just "common sense". Think about the following and then try to keep these ideas in mind when designing your site.

- **Age:** how old are your readers? Are they mostly young, mostly middle-aged, or come from more age groups? Can the language you use with a younger person differ from how you speak to an elderly person? Likewise, you might consider site design / layout, such as increasing the size of text on your website for older visitors.

- **Gender:** is your site primarily for men or mainly for women? It will probably not surprise you to know that the two kinds love different things and respond in different ways. If you have a gender bias on your website, make sure you target; Also, do not design your site to look overly masculine or overly feminine if you target both genders!

- **Location:** the largest online market is the United States, but if you turn to other countries such as Italy, consider the strengths of this country. For example, cooking, fashion, cars, etc.

- **Previous knowledge:** how much do your visitors already know about your topic? Are you throwing them deep, or are you bored with the basics? Are people trying to buy the product "newbies" or more experienced? Choose how to target your content.

- **Expectations:** once you get to your website, what do they expect to find? If there's a big gap between their expectations and what they think you're offering at first glance, they'll click on the Back button and they'll run away from there.

For example: if you expect lessons, do not offer them reviews; if they wait for an informative article, do not hit them with a heavy sales blow.

You could say that you do not care if someone presses the back button immediately - after all, at least some people will stay on the site - but remember that Google looks at your "bounce rate" to see if people are finding useful information on your site. A high rebound frequency can mean lower rankings in search engines. Formulating the "title" tags carefully can help mitigate or prevent them, so make sure they are an accurate representation of the actual content of your page (as you continue to address your keywords!).

- **Needs:** Many affiliates exaggerate by providing information on the background of their product, the history of their product, uses and testimonials for the product, without realizing that all that their customers really want is to look at the product! In contrast, a site could provide images and product specifications galore, but does not realize that their visitors really want reviews and opinions to help make a decision.

Think about what your visitors want and you need to help them make a purchase.

- **Competition:** where could your visitors have previously gone? Make sure your site is up to the competition: clearer designs, more targeted information, offers that your competitors may not have - remember that people do not just visit a website, but look around.

- **Design:** Make sure that the design of your website and the text you use are "appropriate" for your audience. It can be helpful to have a friend or relative to look at your site and see what they think; you can also try to put yourself in the mindset of your audience and look at your site from that perspective. It requires a little imagination, but you will take control of it!

Summary of the lesson

In this lesson we have studied how to find out, what your market wants and how to choose accordingly. A couple of ways you can improve your targeting are as follows:

- Examining search volumes for related keywords, using search engine suggestions or a suitable keyword tool

- Taking a more personal approach and visiting forums for your target market

Once you've identified the best ways to target your keywords, it's also worth taking a look at your site and content and reflecting on the following aspects:

- **Age:** do you have a specific age target?

- **Gender:** is the target audience primarily a specific genre?

- **Location:** where do they come from?

- **Previous knowledge:** what do they already know?

- **Expectation:** what do your visitors expect and is what they get?

- **Needs:** does your site meet the needs of your audience?

- **Competition:** how are the best or different competition sites?

- **Design:** does your site "make sense" for your target?

16.   Understanding of market interactions

As an affiliate you want to maximize your profit, so ideally you want to find markets that are successful both for pay-per-click and for SEO. So the question is: is it still worth selling in a market where you can make money with just one of these methods?

In this lesson we examine **Understanding of market interactions**.

Pay per click does not always work

In general, if you're making a lot of money with pay-per-click you'll also earn money with SEO. However, the opposite is not always true.

For example, the Hair Cut Advice site is very well positioned in search engines and receives many visitors, but only earns from internal advertising. When we tested pay-per-click, the results were bad!

It turns out that even though there are thousands of people looking for keywords to cut their hair, they are not trying to buy. And this means that they very rarely click on the ads.

However this site, which is largely made up of free content, still makes some money through CPA and Google Adsense, so it's not bad at all!

Predict the market

One might wonder if there is a way to predict this situation when doing market research. The answer is YES, to a certain extent.

For example, you can see evidence that the hairstyles market is weighted according to the SEO when looking for the terms "hair cut advice" or "hair style advice" in search engines. There are very few pay-per-click ads on display - yet there are over a million websites containing information and images.

You could find other markets like this at some point; markets with a high number of people looking for keywords, but with a very small pay-per-click advertising.

You should not refuse these markets - most other marketers will do so, so it may be worthwhile to put together a website and earn income from SEO, even if a lower income than you would earn from a market that earns from both pay payments. -per-click and SEO.

SEO is also an alternative position. If you can not profit from pay-per-click but you've done everything on your site, you can still aim to get a lot of traffic and make money this way.

How SEO can help you improve your pay-per-click

The advantage of SEO is that you can experiment with dozens of search terms at no cost, while this is much more expensive with pay-per-click. Even if your website can only rank for a small number of search terms early on, you may find high rankings for long-tail keywords you did not even think about at a later time.

Google Analytics is an essential tool in this situation because it shows all the keywords people have been searching for and leading to your site. Reviewing this information can help you find new search terms to make pay-per-click offers, and there are better chances to be profitable terms.

This strategy is particularly useful if you are testing two or more search results and want to get more visibility for that term.

How pay-per-click can help you improve your SEO

As we learned in previous lessons, pay-per-click can be an expensive learning curve for affiliates, however, if you can afford to invest money, you will find that you can analyze data from your pay-per-click account. enormously advantageous - not only to improve your ads, but also to improve your SEO!

Chances are, if you're making a lot of pay-per-click money, then you'll also make a lot of money on search engine listings.

Approximately 80% of search engine users will click on natural rather than pay-per-click lists, so it's worth transferring information from the pay-per-click market to the website. For example, you might find that "stopping the German shepherd's assault" saves savagely in pay-per-click. Now that you know that this is a key word for success, you can make a big effort to optimize your website for that term and get even on free traffic.

Summary of the lesson

If you can succeed with Pay-Per-Click in a market, you can usually even with search engine optimization, but the opposite is not always true.

You can often find out by doing a quick search and seeing if a keyword is strongly SEO and evaluating different words that bring you results.

However, do not completely ignore the markets that appear to be negative for PPC - many other marketers will do so, which leaves room to build a site to take advantage of the market and get an income (even if small).

17.   7 techniques on how to search for keywords

In this lesson we will discuss 7 valuable techniques and tools to help you develop the best keywords for your niche.

You can have the best affiliate product in the world, but if your buyers can not find your affiliate page, you will not be able to sell a single sock. Here are the keywords: to help direct the people who might want your product to your affiliate site and offers.

The first step is to find out how to use the best super computer ever known, the human brain (in this case yours!), To study ideas. I will therefore provide you with useful sources of inspiration to deepen these initial ideas.

Keyword research can be a time-consuming process, so I'll give you a little advice to classify useful sources. The buyer's intention is an important part of the selection process, to make sure you find the most profitable keywords, so I'll give you some information about this.

Life is always a little bit easier when there is less competition. The keywords are not different, so I'll help you save time by cutting the words with the most competition from your list.

Finally, I'll show you how to bring all your research into a complete keyword list to get the best results when building your website and content.

1. Brainstorm Keyword Ideas manual

One of the most frequently overlooked methods for keyword research is manual brainstorming. You have a big brain ... now put it into practice!

You can use a piece of paper and a pen, but my favorite brainstorming method comes in the form of an online tool called Mind Meister. Let's say we have "Footwear" as a niche. This is the way we would have started our process of creating keywords.

On the first page, you can click on the green "Try a live demo" button to try, or "Start" to subscribe so you can save your ideas.

Now, once you enter, what do you do first? It is necessary to start with the niche and the secondary niches as a basic starting point. After all, when it comes to the topic of what to do for dinner, it is worth starting with what you have available. An obvious starting line is a good thing.

In the case of footwear, place the word itself in the middle.

All the secrets on how to earn from $20,000 to $100,000 per month with Affiliate Programs

So you can easily insert secondary niches by pressing "enter". In this case, we look at phrases like "Sport shoes" or "Women's shoes".

It is important to evaluate your ideas as you progress, eliminating irrelevant options and using relevant combinations where possible. For the sake of this example, we will explore a sub-niche in particular to give us the opportunity to really dig deep. Let's face it, women are generally more crazy about shoes than men, so we'll look at women's shoes to give us lots of options.

The first thing to ask is, what sub-niches are relevant here? With women's shoes in this case, it is likely that "Men's Shoes" is no longer applicable, while "Summer Shoes" may still be.

So, what types of products or services are available in your sub-niche? In this case, for example, I could wear shoes with high heels or casual low shoes next to women's shoes.

Simply select the "women's shoes" bubble and click on "Shift" and "Tab" together to insert the branches.

Finally, use the name of your sub-niche to create branches of keywords on related sub-niches. In this case, with the sub-niche of women's shoes, on the relative sub-niche of summer shoes, I could put "Women's summer shoes" to create a new keyword that is still relevant. Adding one of the original sub-niche branches will give you an even more specific keyword, in this case, "Casual summer shoes for women".

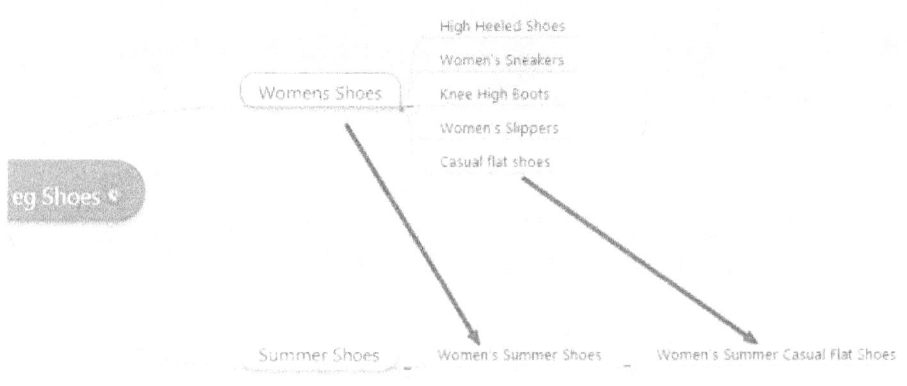

2. Search for inspiration by seed keywords

So you have a few basic words and phrases in your brainstorming and you're ready to create a more in-depth seed keyword list. We have some great tips on where to look.

If you already have products like Clickbank in mind, look at their sales pages. If you do not have products in mind, look at the most popular sales pages in your own niche on websites like Clickbank or look at Amazon for physical products.

Looking at the shoes on Amazon, if I select "Sort by: New and Bestseller" in the upper right corner, I get a list of shoes that are the best sellers.

All the secrets on how to earn from $20,000 to $100,000 per month with Affiliate Programs

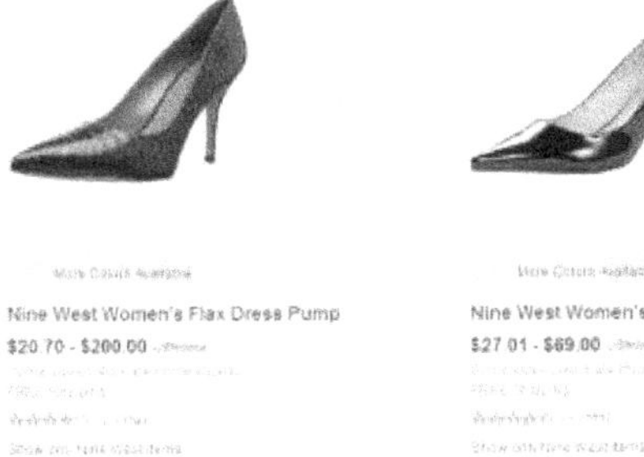

Nine West Women's Flax Dress Pump
$20.70 - $200.00

Nine West Women's Austin Pump
$27.01 - $69.00

Life Stride Women's Parigi Pump
$15.99 - $65.00

The list also contains suggestions on well-functioning products in my sub-niche. "Nove West" seems to be a well-liked brand for example, and "pumps" is a descriptive word that potential customers might look for.

Let's say I looked at the sales page for this particular product.

I learn that "Peep-Toe Pump" is a type of product. This could be a seed keyword for this product. Scrolling down, I can search in the product description to find phrases like "trend-right footwear" or "semi-wrapped platform".

Below, I can see customer reviews. This is great for seeing what problems people have with products in this niche and what they have found as a solution.

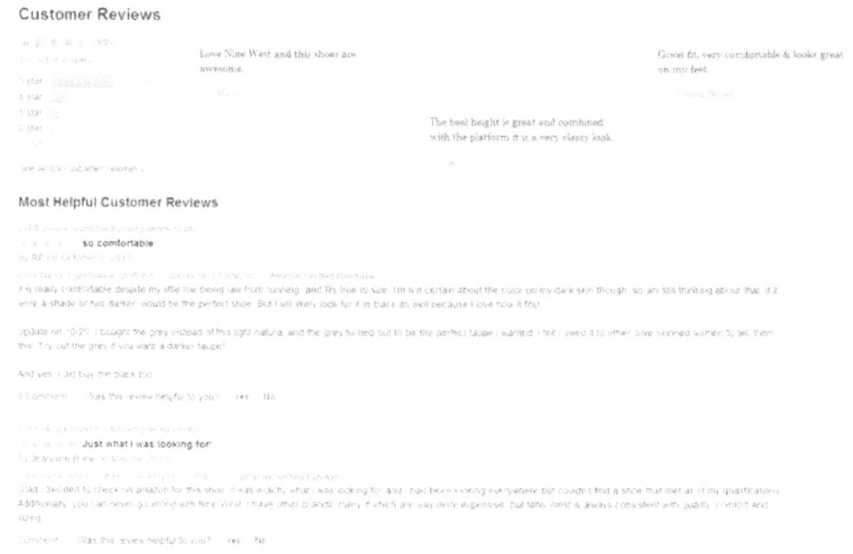

Customers appreciate comfort, so "comfortable shoes" could be a good keyword.

Google is another place to look for inspiration. Typing your brainstorm's words into a Google search will show you the best pages for those words. Take a look at some of them and look at what words or what language they use.

When you search with Google, you'll be shown "related searches" at the bottom of the page.

Searches related to casual flat shoes

casual **flats**	casual **boots**
casual **ballet flats**	casual flat shoes **for men**
casual flat **boots**	flat **sandal** shoes
casual **ballet** shoes	**airflex** shoes

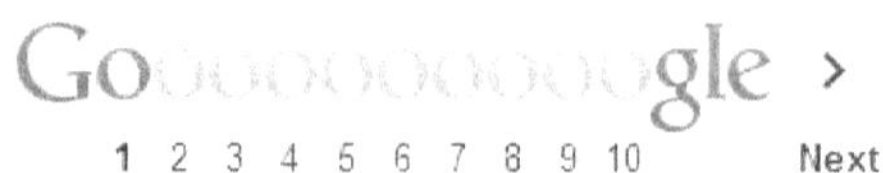

1 2 3 4 5 6 7 8 9 10   Next

This is a really smart, fast and simple way to get relevant and popular seed keywords that maybe you did not even know they were there. Looking for "casual flat shoes" from my initial brainstorm has given me the term "casual dancers" as a popular related research, so I can add it to keywords.

While you're conducting research on Google, try adding "forums" at the beginning to search for forums where people are discussing your niche. The words of wide niche will be more successful in the search for in-depth forums.

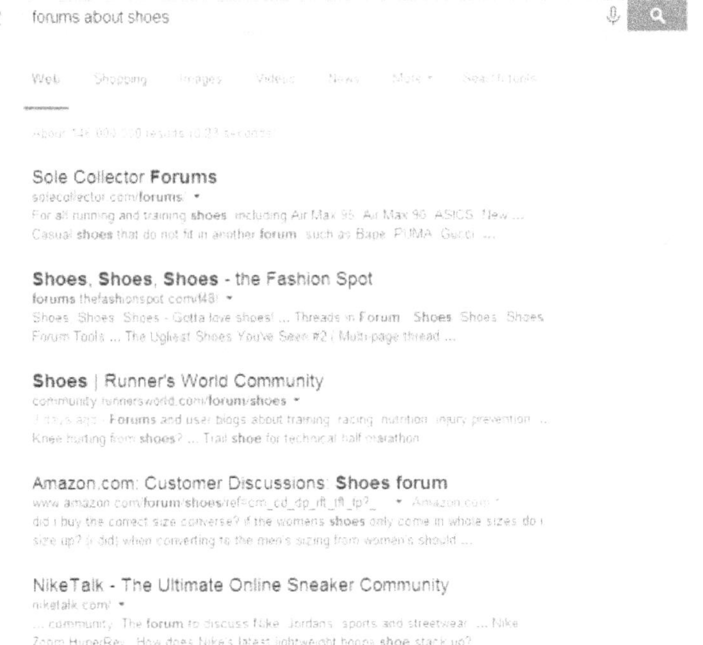

The phrase "forum on shoes" has a lot of results, but consider if your niche could have hot topics or sub-niches that could have their forums.

Replacing "forum on" with "Questions and Answers" will provide you with a similar set of sources of relevant customer reviews. Forums and pages of questions and answers are incredible sources to find popular terms and phrases related to your niche, as well as problems that seek answers.

Creating the best seed keyword list based on the variety of information you find from these sources will give you a real boost in the next steps of this lesson.

Keywords are not enough on their own, but having a wider range of quality keywords offers the best chance at a later time when it comes to processing them in what you really want: the list of winning keywords.

3. Save the juicy keyword sources

While browsing through these forums and discussions, you will find that some are better than others as sources for searching for current keywords. If they are constantly active, they will always have the latest language and terms launched in your niche, which is what you want for building your seed keyword.

If you used MindMeister for your brainstorming, you will see that it has an option for inserting links or files. When you have the branch that the link refers to the most selected, go to the menu on the right.

Make sure you have selected the blue arrow pointing to the right, to insert the link in the box under "URL". Make sure your bubble is checked - in this case I go with "shoe forum" - click on "URL" to make the link appear as the arrow surrounded on the edge of your bubble.

Now, every time you look at your brainstorming for inspiration from updated seed keywords, simply click on the most relevant link to your new product, offer or content.

4. Do not ignore the buyer's intention

It's easy to be swept only with high-volume keyword targeting. But you should not ignore the buyer's intent. So what does it involve?

The keywords for the buyer are words or phrases that include an indication of a sale. In other words, adding words or phrases like "buy" or "lower prices" at the beginning of a keyword usually means that people are navigating with that keyword to buy.

You should avoid using only the keywords that catch the attention of the conversation or social media, and instead find out what will get the most hits on sales at the end of the scale.

For example, those looking for "shoes" could simply search for general information. Someone who seeks "the best price for shoes" is practically grabbing the wallet awaiting the purchase of what he is looking for.

Keywords with buyer intent often have lower competition because they have less search volume than generic words. But in theory they have a much higher conversion rate when they are researched and this makes them a very valuable resource to explore.

Look at the buyer's perspective, check your keyword list and add any missing transactional keywords.

5. Use the tools to generate long-tail keywords
As with the buyer's intent, the more specific your keywords are, the more likely you are to get people who actually want your product. This is where the long-tail keywords arrive.

You can use tools like Ubersuggest to develop a list of highly targeted long-tailed keywords. I'll show you how easy it can be.

With Ubersuggest: just enter the relevant details, then click on suggest.

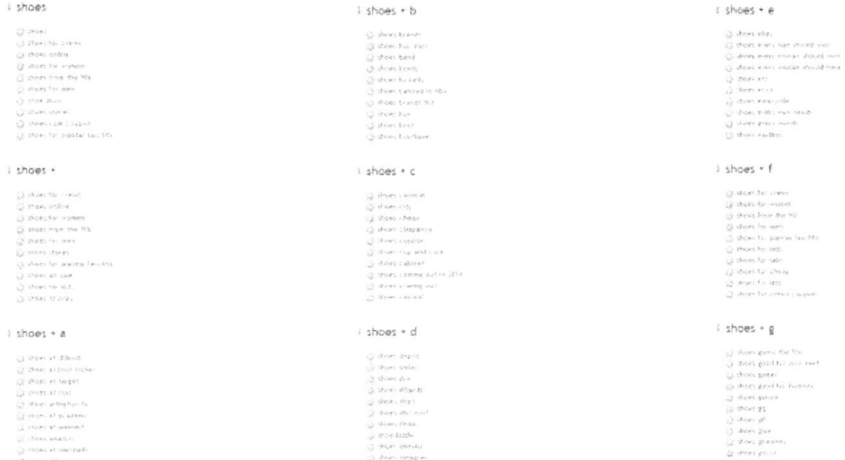

And there you are, generated lists of keywords that people are looking for in relation to your words.

At this point, you can search for content. Get the phrases that appear from a search and then add them to the search box to get even more ideas.

Keep a list of all the data of your keywords by exporting them to CSV so you can organize them later. By the end of this phase, you should have a fairly large inventory of relevant keywords. So, out of that multitude, which ones do you really want to use?

All the secrets on how to earn from $20,000 to $100,000 per month with Affiliate Programs

6. Filter high-competition keywords

This is where the filtering process comes into play. We have further expanded our list to get the best possible scope, and now it's time to perfect true quality. With Traffic Travis, it is easy to determine the search competition for each given keyword.

When Traffic Travis is loaded, make sure you have selected the SEO tab, then choose the Competition option in it.

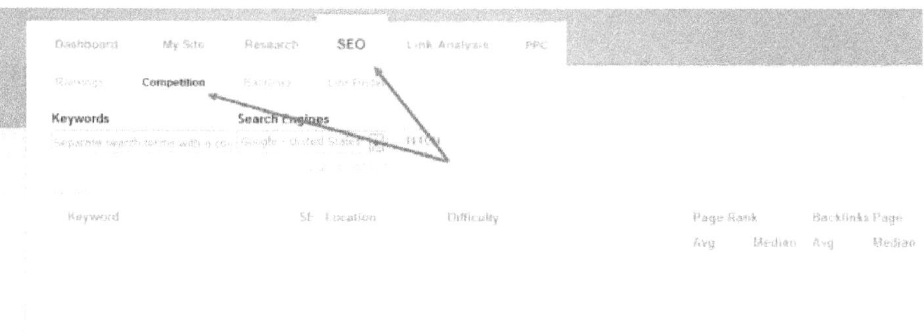

Click the Keywords text box and a small window will appear in which you can enter keywords.

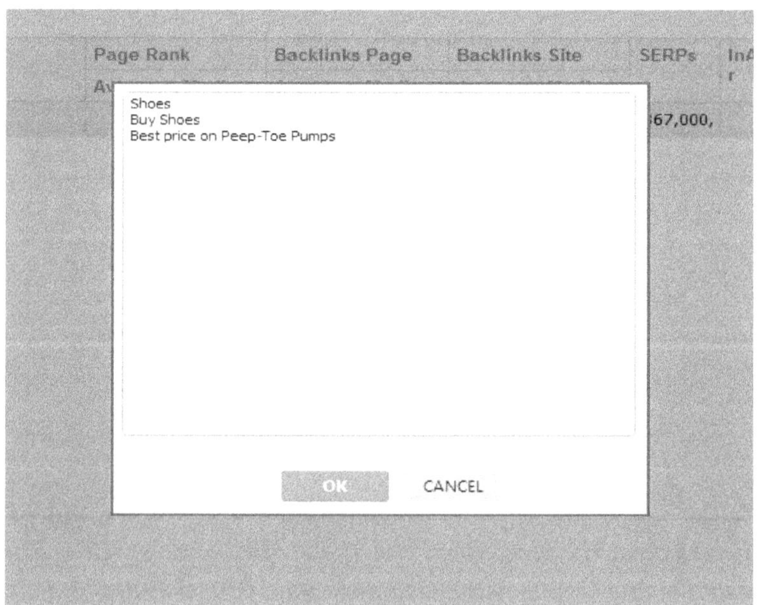

Copy and paste the words into groups, click "ok" and let the search make its own example! You can then see the difficulty levels of different words.

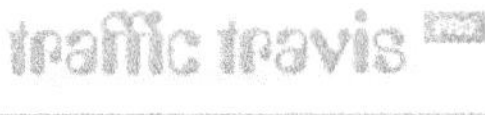

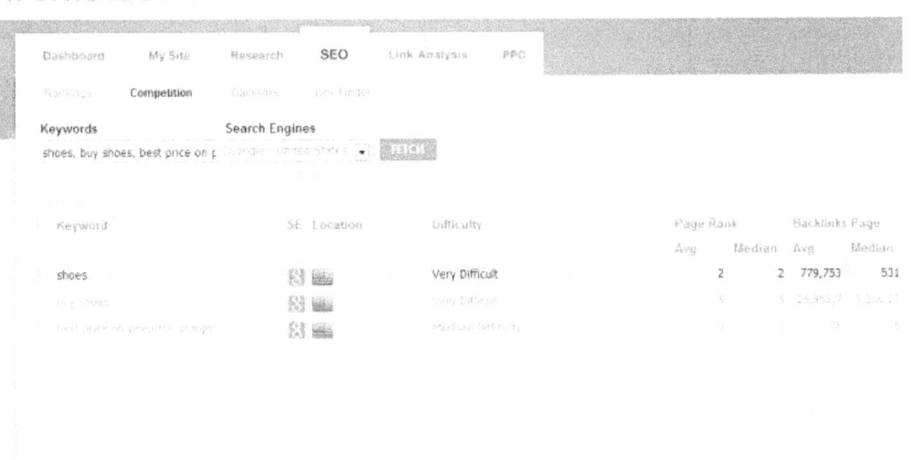

"Shoes" and "buying shoes" are very general, so it makes sense that they have a "very difficult" result, while "the best price for peep-toe pumps" is a bit more specific and has a medium difficulty.

You can delete words with "high difficulty" whenever possible, especially if you are a new affiliate, as it is unlikely that you will get a sufficiently high ranking.

Be sure to export these search results to CSV so you can organize them later.

7. Make your final keyword selections

Now that you've eliminated low search volumes and unwanted competition, it's time to create a list of key keywords consisting of the best 30 or 40 keywords for an initial site.

Remember, the higher the search volume and the lower the competition, so make your selections with this in mind. Those transactional keywords are the most important after that initial rule, due to their higher level of potential profit.

A good way to put everything into perspective is to think about searching for keywords like selling apples from an orchard. If you go and collect the first ones you meet on the ground, it is likely that they will be half-march and nobody will buy them.

You have to collect the entire orchard and put the apples through a quality filtering process.

It might seem like a lot of work for the same amount of keywords, but the quality difference is what it could make or not make at this stage of your affiliate strategy.

With this in mind, you've worked for these results! Be sure to use them to guide content creation and marketing efforts in the future. Use a maximum of 5 keywords per page.

One last tip for your keyword strategy is to use only the number of keywords per page that you can naturally insert into your content without spam or lists. If you're just pumping the page full of keywords, put out search engines and people and they will not come back to your site.

Conclusion

So that's it! I showed you how to develop your keywords. We started brainstorming using MindMeister, and then we developed our sources of inspiration to save for later. We have emphasized the importance of buyer's intent or "transactional keywords" in the keyword research process.

With the keyword list seed up and running, we have expanded the quality and variety of keywords with tools like Ubersuggest. Traffic Travis then helped us eliminate the words of high competition, ending with our selection of final keywords.

18. How to use Facebook

Social media is where people from every corner of the globe connect on the Internet, so it's important to spread the word that your site or affiliate offer is what they need to be watched! First of all, we will discover the marketing potential of Facebook and why it is so important to use it as a tool in your affiliate strategy. We will then see how to set up your page so you can use Facebook to expand your marketing coverage.

Once you've set everything up, you need to make sure your Facebook page is designed for SEO, so I'll explain how to do it. "Like" is the social currency of Facebook, so I'll teach you how to use this system to grow the number of relevant people who "like" your page.

As you develop this fan base, you need to engage with them, both to keep your Facebook page active, and to grow your social media. I will guide you through the best ways to do it. All this creates traffic for Facebook, but to make it relevant to your marketing, you need to report traffic to your affiliate sites and offers. Last but not least, I'll tell you how Facebook ads work and show you how to make them.

Why Facebook?

Facebook is the number one social network, with over a billion people using it all over the world. The flow of information that spreads on Facebook every day is a hive of potential that you, as a marketing affiliate, need to draw on to spread the knowledge of your affiliate site or your offers.

When other Facebook users appreciate what they see, they have a simple and easy way to show it. By clicking on "Like", they are showing on their feed that it is there and that they approve. They can also click on "Share" to re-publish it on their wall or even on a friend's wall. This can be seen by their friends, and if their friends like it, the same process happens again. In the end, you end up with a chain effect, which starts from your page and spreads, reaching a multitude of relevant people.

One of the best things about this process is that your social coverage grows by including relevant people who are more likely to be interested for two reasons. First of all, it is more likely that the friends of those who liked the post will have similar interests to those of random people on the Internet. If a friend liked your topic, it is likely that it could also be what they are interested in.

Secondly, the post gets a certain level of value and trust among these friends of fans, when they see that someone they are friends with has put their appreciation on it by clicking "like".

All of these are serious reasons why you can not afford to overlook Facebook as a powerful tool in your affiliate marketing strategy.

Setting up your Facebook page
If you do not already have a Facebook page, you'll be wondering how to get started. Do not worry, it's easy and fast to set up your personal page, and I'm here to guide you.

In this purely hypothetical example, Marco Rossi runs a site called "Lose weight naturally" and wants to promote it via a Facebook page. Follow, keep your niche in mind and make selections based on what works for you.

First, go to Facebook and access your personal profile. If you do not already have one, be sure to create an account so that you can continue with the creation of your affiliate page.

Once you are logged in, click the wheel at the top right of the screen and click on the first option, "Create a page". This will take you to a page that shows you all the categories you will choose from. In the case of Marco, he will click on the "Trademark or product" page and scroll down to "website".

This is where you enter the name of your website or product promotion, remembering to keep it short and snappy. Do not try to fill it with keywords. Keep in mind that for SEO purposes the first word will have more influence on Google than the other words in your title. In this example, Mark could choose "Lose weight in just two weeks" to be effective.

Then there are three cards to be processed. The first concerns the creation of the about section. For SEO purposes this is a great place to put keywords, but not just list them. Use them in a couple of sentences that will best describe your topic. In the case of Marco could put "Lose weight in just two weeks with natural products! Get now a promotion on www.perderepeso.com."

So simply enter the name of your website below, and answer the question, is your page topic a real product or trademark? For the sake of this example, I'll click "no", but feel free to click "yes" if yours is.

Then you will enter your profile picture, either from your computer or from your website. Be sure to keep the representative image the same on Facebook as well as on your website so that traffic from A to B can quickly and easily identify that your website is actually where they were trying to go.

As a last option you can choose to promote your page, using Facebook's internal advertising system. If you have the funds to do it, this is definitely something to be reckoned with. However, do not be in a hurry, as you can opt for this at any time, not just in the initial setup phase.

SEO for your Facebook page

So you have a page. You kept SEO in mind when you created it. It's time to look at some other actions you can take to ensure good SEO for your Facebook page. Once your page has reached 25 likes, you have the option to create a custom URL.

Search engines attach importance to URLs, so keep them relevant based on the name of your brand or affiliate website. For example, the Facebook URL in this case could be www.facebook.com/perderepeso, so that it is easy for search engines and interested people to understand and find.

Just like with any other website, backlinking is another great way to increase the SEO of your Facebook page.

Use status updates to regularly provide search engines with the keywords they need to identify your posts and then the page. Just like the name of your page, Google attributes the most value to the first word, so we recommend setting it as a keyword whenever possible.

Google will use the first 180 characters of your status updates as a meta description, so try to keep short and quick status updates. Including a direct link to your affiliate site in your posts is a great idea so you can drive Facebook traffic to your website.

The Facebook "notes" rank well in search engines and represent a widely used opportunity for traffic. They are particularly useful for expanding special offers or events. You can create one by clicking "Notes" in the Apps section, located in the left sidebar on the Facebook home page.

Get sympathies

The page is now running and is set for SEO. It's time to talk about managing your Facebook page with the goal of getting I like engaging. Getting lots of likes is important for growing your followers and creating a strong foundation for that multiplier effect.

You need to use Like to make the multiplier work. This means people who will follow your page and will continue to click Like and share your content and updates with their friends.

To get started: if you have a list of emails from your affiliate website, send an email to let them know that you now have a Facebook page and kindly invite them to verify it. Let them know that if they want to receive updates when they find interesting information about your niche, they should "like" your page. Be careful not to be intrusive. Give your readers information, but do not tell them what to do.

Having a Facebook badge on your affiliate website or on another page shows visitors that your Facebook page exists. This is another way to grow your number of likes, making sure that your Facebook page attracts the attention of people who already approve your site. Check out the Facebook Plug-ins to learn more about how to add a Facebook badge to your site.

Avoid buying like. They will ruin your page because none of them will "like" or "share" your posts. They're more like a dead weight, and it makes it seem like none of your fans are interested in you, and I can assure you that you notice right away.

This can affect the scope of your updates, preventing your real fans from seeing the content you share. You need to be liked by people who will interact with you and transmit your content to other real people, and the way to get it is to have quality content.

This is very important, so I'll see which elements make it fun, shareable or funny. As we examine it, I want you to think about what your topic, theme or niche is and what elements are or are not relevant to that audience.

Whether the media that you publish are images, videos or text, must have a core of emotions with which your audience can relate. Think about what would be attractive to your target audience.

Comedy is a great way to brighten up the day. On the Internet, it usually takes the form of images or short videos. Make sure you're in good taste and appeal to the kind of humor you think the people you're talking to would be interested.

Cuteness is also loved on the internet. The photos and videos of cats in particular are everywhere.

Stories of engaging or post-controversial news stories can raise people up, but be careful not to use anything that may reflect badly on your brand. Finally, the inspirational posts are a panacea and spread easily on Facebook.

You can also produce educational posts, such as the latest scientific news, or an article that belies popular current myths floating on social media websites. Lists like "The 10 songs of the 90s" or "How to train a cat in 5 steps" are also good.

Addictive with the fans

So getting interesting likes is one thing, but keeping them is another. And it's the most important thing. You must interact with your fans regularly. Keep the quality of your posts high. Do not publish too much, do not publish too little. You need to do your right amount of post.

Unless you have a news page, 1 to 4 messages in a week are a good goal depending on how heavy your content is. With this, I mean if your posts tend to be news or light entertainment, more frequent publishing is a better option. With heavier posts like videos or links to articles, once a week is enough.

Keep yourself optimistic, maintaining a style of content that viewers expect. For example, the style of your posts must be catchy and appropriate, and the content must have value for fans.

Use apps creatively so that your target audience of Facebook can interact with you. Create surveys, such as "how long you want to lose weight". This is also a good way to get people to comment on your posts, because the question posts have an average of 100% more comments than posts not being discussed.

Also create games and quizzes. People love them and often redirect the results of a quiz to their page. People also like free products, so create exclusive offers and promotions on Facebook. For example, you could say "To 100 shares of this post, I offer good purchase for ...." "Or gift ...."

Direct Facebook traffic to the affiliate / offer page

Now it's time to get to work. You can accumulate fascinating sympathies and a large Facebook audience, but as an affiliate this does not mean anything until you get that traffic on your website and offers, and then sell.

It is better to think about how to filter to build the relationship you want rather than to spam promotional bullets. An 80% ratio of entertainment content and 20% promotion helps you build that relationship so you can market your affiliate site without moving people away.

Make sure that what you're promoting is your affiliate site rather than a direct sale. It's better at this point to turn traffic into leads that are familiar with your website, so that more people are interested in going there to see your content, whether it's a blog post or a blog post. article, or even a special deal.

Once you've captured an audience with an enticing reason to come back to your site, send it to a compression page so you can get it on your email list. This will allow you to expand your affiliate marketing strategy from Facebook to your site with inclusion in email marketing, which is important for you to create as an affiliate. As they say, "**Money is on the list**!"

Advertising on Facebook
Another way to get a portion of the massive Facebook user base on your Facebook page, affiliate site, or offers is to use Facebook Ads. Facebook ads are a bit like pay-per-click advertising, but there is also an option to pay for 1000 impressions (CPM).

They help you target specific audiences because Facebook has information about ages, places and what their general interests are, so you have targeted advertising. This is useful for speeding up traffic to a fast offer if you have the budget to do it. Let's take a quick look at the set up for Facebook ads.

You'll find an option to create an ad from your personal Facebook account in the drop-down menu that appears when you click on the small wheel in the upper right corner.

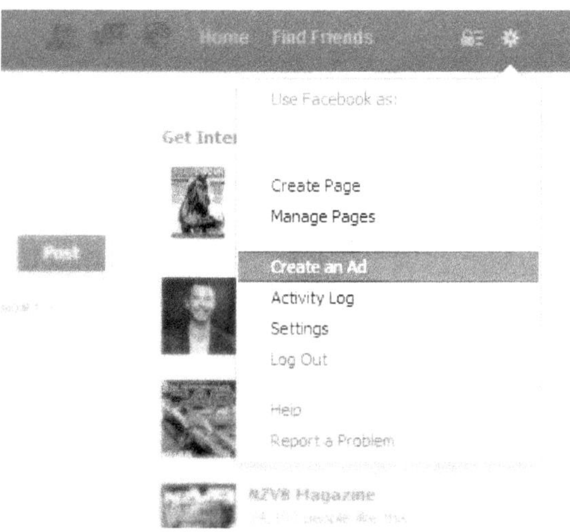

There are a selection of options to meet different goals. If you want more people to interact with your page, choose the option above, or for the page I like that you select the one below. To send them to a compression page, try website conversions so that you can track how many clicks are converted to email registrations.

Advertise on Facebook

Help: Choosing an Objective

What kind of results do you want for your ads?

- Page Post Engagement
- Page Likes
- Clicks to Website
- Website Conversions
- App Installs
- App Engagement
- Event Responses
- Offer Claims

To get them in the content or offers of your website, try Clicking on the website, once you add your website you can add images. Try to focus on six images in order to have a different range and follow the recommended image size of 600 by 315 pixels.

The next step in the process allows you to link your ad to your Facebook page. The link is still transferred to the website, but this gives a little more advertising to your page and helps to create the association between your Facebook page and your site. You can also add a call-to-action button if you have one.

Make sure that when you create the title and text in the lower-left sections, choose snappy phrases, "lose weight in two weeks" to be as effective as possible with your own page.

This next bit is important for making your ads the right people. What is the target market for your affiliate site? Add places, ages, gender, languages and interests to make sure your ad is specific enough to hit the best audience. You can even add additional demographics with the drop-down box below the languages.

Use advanced connection targeting to reach only people with certain characteristics. The indicator at the top right will tell you how wide or specific your search is. On a lower budget, you must be as specific as possible. If you have a high budget you can afford to expand it more.

All the secrets on how to earn from $20,000 to $100,000 per month with Affiliate Programs

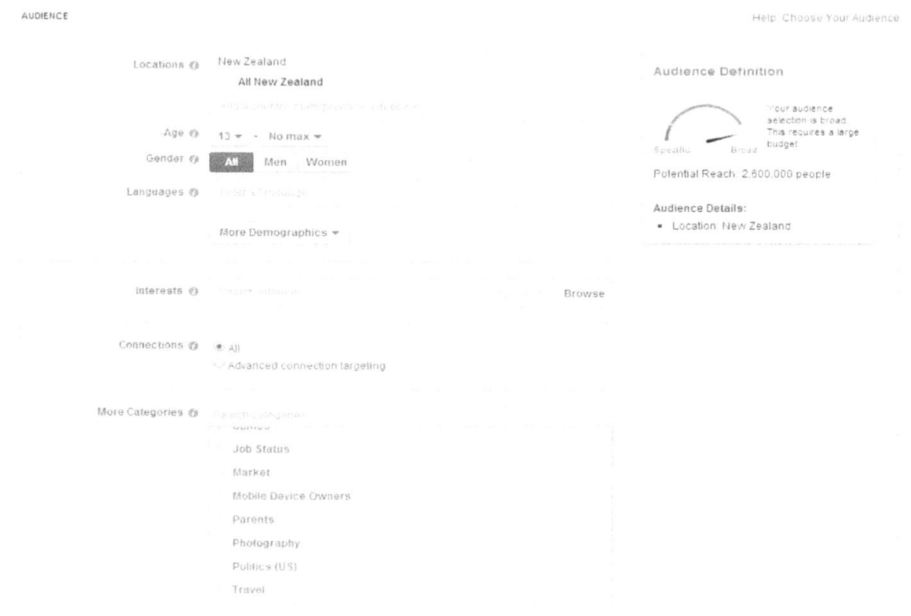

Finally, you enter the account settings, including currency, country and time zone. Set the budget, such as the X amount of euros per day, then set the ad to run continuously or start and end on specific dates.

The Facebook ads shown are decided based on a number of factors, including market competition, target audience, and ad performance history. In the Offers and prices section, you can automatically optimize the bid to get more clicks.

This is useful to ensure that your offer is not set too low for the ad to show, but also that you do not pay more for an impression or click of the necessary.

All the secrets on how to earn from $20,000 to $100,000 per month with Affiliate Programs

ACCOUNT AND CAMPAIGN

Help: Campaign

Account Settings

These settings cannot be changed once you create your ad.

Account Currency

Account Country

Account Time Zone

Campaign and Budget

Name

Budget Per day ▼

Schedule • Run my campaign continuously starting today
Set a start and end date

BIDDING AND PRICING

Help: Bidding and Pricing

Bidding Bid for clicks ▼

Pricing Your bid will be optimized to get more clicks on your ad. You will be charged every time someone is shown your ad.
* Automatically optimize your bid to get more clicks
Manually set your maximum bid for clicks (CPC)

Review Order

Conclusion

So that's it! An entire guide to using Facebook as an affiliate, why you should use it first, until you create your SEO and likes pages, as well as engage your fans to drive traffic to your affiliate site and offers. We also discovered Facebook advertising.

The main thing to remember is to keep up with quality and regular posts that are not spam, but to encourage the public to genuinely appreciate what you are trying to show them. So use your quality guide hooks and, if you can afford it, Facebook ads, to bring traffic back to your website.

19.   How to use Twitter

To teach you everything about using Twitter as an affiliate, we'll cover a wide range of topics to help you succeed!

We start by driving through what is Twitter, to know why you should use it and what you can do there. So we make it super simple by guiding you through the movements of your personal profile. This way you have no reason not to try!

Let's find out how to make those tweets work and then what to put to get attention in the vast chorus of tweets on Twitter.

Let's find out how to get more followers for the maximum impact of tweets. Ultimately, all this social support is to help you with a strategy that relates to your affiliate goals, so we find out how to bring the fruits of your work - that is, your followers - back to your affiliate website and offers.

So let's try to understand why you can not afford not to use Twitter and what you can really do.

Introduction to Twitter
Basically, it's huge. The Twitter user base is really impressive. Second only to Facebook, it has more than 300 million unique monthly visitors estimated.

1 | Facebook
3 - eBizMBA Rank | **900,000,000** - Estimated Unique Monthly Visitors | 3 - Compete Rank | 3 - Quantcast Rank | 2 - Alexa Rank
The Most Popular Social Networking Sites | eBizMBA

2 | Twitter
14 - eBizMBA Rank | **310,000,000** - Estimated Unique Monthly Visitors | 25 - Compete Rank | 5 - Quantcast Rank | 11 - Alexa Rank
The Most Popular Social Networking Sites | eBizMBA

Twitter is very simple: the short messages that people exchange are easy and people love this simple exchange to share information with each other, so you can get a great benefit even by using for only 15 minutes a day .

The messages on Twitter are called "tweets" and you can send them to your followers and to the general public. They have a limit of 280 characters, so it is easy to produce many in a short space of time.

Twitter allows people to follow others' tweets when they encounter something they like. You will use it to get regular traffic on your Twitter account and, of course, on your affiliate website.

It looks pretty good, right? Let's find out how to create your Twitter account to allow you to get your Tweet.

How to start with Twitter

Go to Twitter and sign up for an account. Fill in all the required details, such as name, email address, username and password.

Once entered, enter the details on your page. Do this to make sure your Twitter profile is accessible and easy to understand for other Twitter users who may be interested in your affiliate website.

Your "Information" section is also a good place to enter keywords, as well as the URL of your affiliate site, because people can search for you based on what words your biography contains.

Do not forget to add a profile picture. Make sure this is relevant to your brand, so that you can easily identify yourself on your website when Twitter followers follow it. (use the same image used for Facebook and the site)

When you have the profile set up, following other people tweeting content that is relevant to your niche is a great way to draw attention to your new Twitter profile, so make sure you find some.

Just type in the keywords from your niche in the search bar, select if you want to examine the profiles or bios and click on the "Follow" button.

Followerwonk provides you with a list of Twitter users related to your keyword. You can see and sort according to how many tweets tweeted, how many people are following, how many followers they have, how long they are active on Twitter and their social authority.

Now that you need to recruit followers, you also need to give them something to read, and that's where your tweets arrive.

How to tweet

So, how is this story of Tweeting done? Publishing a Tweet is very simple. Just click on the "Twitta" box on the right side of the screen and enter the text. Once you have entered the text, click on the blue "Twitta" button and it's done!

On Twitter, placing the hash symbol (#) before a word or phrase uses the so-called "hashtag". This allows people interested in the keyword to see your tweets, whether they follow you or not. Not even the hashtags must be at the beginning or end of your tweet. You can place them anywhere in your sentence.

If you click on a hashtag word, you'll see that other tweets are also tagged with that keyword. This is how non-followers with relevant interests can find you and, just as importantly, how you can find them.

Be careful not to send spam to all tweets with too many hashtags. The use of more than two is excessive. Focus only on the most relevant words to make sure your tweets reach their mark.

The great thing about this is that it spreads your reach by allowing their followers to make their way through the Tweet. Most Twitter users continually incorporate links into their tweets, and it's a good chance that you link back to your affiliate site or your offer.

Write better tweets

Your Tweets are your voice here, so it's essential to make them high quality. Why? The cycle of social media. Big tweets get more followers. A greater number of followers leads to a higher level of social media involvement. This commitment is what ultimately leads to traffic. The tests show that the best titles are what draws attention to the huge mass of tweets that fly around every day. You can increase the conversion rate on a 73% website or link and make sure your title is convincing.

Make it relevant to your niche and really try to get into the head of your audience to produce a title that you would click on. The first thing is to master the art of maximum impact in minimal space. You only have 280 characters. Make sure you have 10 seconds to get someone's attention, it's an effective method.

Every time you write a tweet, do you think: do you have all the information, hashtags and links I need, nothing more and nothing less? "Keep as fast and interesting as possible by including only what you need.

How to get more followers

So you've created your links to your Twitter page, affiliate site or Ri-Tweetable offers. Now you just have to give your followers a reason to want to share your tweet.

While Tweeting is the language, the followers are the population and you want as many faithful as possible.

Resist the temptation to go and buy followers on Twitter. They will probably be fake or non-reactive accounts and you could end up being banned, which is the last thing you want for your brand.

Announce that you have Twitter on your affiliate site and that people should follow you for up-to-date content.

Find those relevant people via their tweets and websites like Followerwonk. Be careful not to be overzealous with this though, because if you follow more people the amount of followers you have, you run the risk of losing authority. Be selective to become a more influential personality.

Target more influential personalities and interact with them in addition to your suite. Participate in their conversations. Try to add something useful and interesting or to show appreciation if they have an interesting Tweet. Above all, focus on selecting those with a big influence in your niche on Twitter.

To avoid slipping off your new followers' radar, you must publish regular tweets. Try to bet at least 1 or 2 tweets a day to show that your account is active.

Strategies Tweet

The general strategy of using Twitter as an affiliate is to drive traffic to your affiliate site through social media interactions, and the key is a smooth, seamless patient transition.

Twitter is for social interaction, your affiliate site is for sale. Use Twitter as bait to bring them back to your site, not just a hook to capture them in a direct sale. If they see a hook, they do not bite.

Link to quality testimonials, blog posts or other to bring them to your affiliate site, as well as other valuable information they might be interested in. Always tell people what you're connecting to, though. Nobody likes to be deceived and if the link goes to something different or poor quality, it will not exactly be your biggest fan.

If a followers engages with you, make sure to respond as quickly as possible, thanks to them your page grows, ask them questions to keep a dialogue on something genuine. No one is trying to be a robot friend, so be as humane as possible to build the best relationship with your audience.

Tweeta when your followers are actually online to guarantee the best interaction possibilities. You can check what are your most watched hours online on Followerwonk and also when you need to be active.

For example, if your niche is physical fitness, Followerwonk Analysis shows that your Twitter contacts tend to get online between 17:00 and 19:00, they are likely to be looking for the motivation for their training routine after work.

This means that you need to post around 17:00 for maximum exposure.

Conclusion
We have seen the various stages of Twitter, how to set up your profile and get tweeting. We shared information on how to write the best tweets to captivate audiences, then create your own base of followers, not to mention the final strategies for transforming your use of social media into successful affiliation.

20.   The importance of e-mail Marketing

How important is email marketing?
It is very important to have an email list for affiliate marketing, I would say **FUNDAMENTAL**! Several affiliates earn thousands of dollars just from their email marketing.

Although you can earn good money simply with "traffic brokerage", that is: by promoting a product, earning a commission in a sale and leaving it at that point, I can tell you that you have not seen anything comparable to the profit you could make with a newsletter.

To give you an idea of the power of email marketing: most marketers find that adding a series of newsletters automatically doubles their income; in fact, it is not uncommon for people to increase their income up to five times!

Mark Ling says that a recently sent newsletter e-mail earned him a quarter of a million dollars in 4 days; for regular promotions, you will easily receive $ 10,000 in sales from a single email.

Another major internet seller, Frank Kern, claims to have earned over 1 million dollars in less than 4 hours from a single email. If these figures do not attract your attention, then nothing will do it.

Why is email marketing so immensely profitable?

Email marketing is so immensely profitable because, in effect, it allows you to make continuous sales to proven buyers. (already interested in your products)

You worked so hard to attract visitors to your site, it seems a shame to miss this big opportunity! A newsletter list allows you to keep in touch with a huge proportion of visitors to your site. And it allows you to keep selling them for months, if not even years. And to these are constantly added others.

Another huge advantage of a newsletter is that you can also use it to promote new products being launched. This is a very effective way to increase enthusiasm, so on the day of launch, your subscribers will automatically buy your product. A typical product launch can be profitable, but without an e-mail list, you will lose many already secure gains.

Types of newsletters: online or email only

The products you are promoting will determine which type of newsletter will work best. There are two types:

1. **The online newsletter:** it is here that you send a short email newsletter containing a short introduction followed by a link, which the reader must click to read the rest of the content. The advantage of an online newsletter is that you can make it look good with good graphics and layout. And, more importantly, it allows you to host video and audio, which is very important for topics like "learn the guitar" or "learn Spanish".

2. **The alternative is the e-mail newsletter** - the e-mail newsletters indicate that the complete text is contained in the e-mail itself. In general, I prefer to use this style of newsletter simply because otherwise, with every action you ask people to take, you lose people - when you get there, people are lazy! So, as a general rule, e-mail newsletters get more readers.

By saying this, some topics are better suited to online newsletters, as we have already said, especially the topics that require multimedia to be more effective.

Finally, there is also a third type of email, which is a sort of hybrid between the online newsletter and the blog. If you have a blog, you may want to publish a "live newsletter", where the newsletters are the posts of your blog and send a short e-mail containing a teaser and a link every time you add a new post. This is what I do and I found it an effective way to attract more readers to the blog.

Summary of the lesson
In this lesson, you learned how much email marketing is extremely profitable for affiliates and why the type of email you send depends on whether you're promoting media or not.

CONCLUSION

We came to the conclusion of this guide, I hope I gave you all the information you needed to start this new business. I know that now you will want to start immediately to put into practice what I have told you, and it is also right. But again, do not skip the steps that I explained to you, choose calmly the "niche" to work on because it is VERY IMPORTANT. You lose a bit of time so you will not have any problems later, I've been there long before you and I know what it means to waste time at the beginning and not immediately achieve results.

With this I greet you and I wish you so much SUCCESS and MONEY ☺

www.ingramcontent.com/pod-product-compliance
Lightning Source LLC
Chambersburg PA
CBHW061517250726
48657CB00005B/1922